Come Back, Barbara

Also by C. John Miller

Outgrowing the Ingrown Church
    (available from Zondervan)
Repentance and Twentieth Century Man
Evangelism and Your Church
A New Life
Completely Forgiven

Come Back, Barbara

Foreword by
LAWRENCE J. CRABB, Jr.

C. JOHN MILLER &
BARBARA MILLER JULIANI

Zondervan Books
Zondervan Publishing House
Grand Rapids, Michigan

COME BACK, BARBARA
Copyright © 1988 by C. John Miller and Barbara Miller Juliani

Zondervan Books
are published by Zondervan Publishing House
1415 Lake Drive, S.E.
Grand Rapids, MI 49506

Library of Congress Cataloging in Publication Data

Miller, C. John.
   Come back, Barbara / C. John Miller and Barbara Miller Juliani.
      p. cm.
   ISBN 0-310-37471-5
   1. Miller, C. John. 2. Juliani, Barbara Miller. 3. Christian
biography—United States. 4. Fathers and daughters. 5. Family-Reli-
gious life. I. Juliani, Barbara Miller. II. Title.
BR1700.2.M52 1988
248.8'421'0924—dc 192
[B]   88–11924
                                                                   CIP

Unless otherwise noted, all Scripture references are taken from the Holy
Bible: New International Version (North American Edition), copyright © 1973, 1978, 1984 by the International Bible Society. Used by
permission of Zondervan Bible Publishers.

To protect the identity of the innocent and the not-so-innocent, fictional
names are occasionally used.

Printed in the United States of America

   91   92   93   94   95 / CH / 10   9   8   7   6   5   4   3

To our family
who always welcomed Barbara:
Rose Marie, Jim and Roseann, Jim and Ruth,
Paul and Jill, Angelo, Bob and Keren

And to the larger Christian family
who prayed for her so faithfully

Contents

Foreword by Lawrence J. Crabb

Either I'm jaded or there aren't many books coming out that break new ground. Most good books are fresh reminders or clearer statements of important truths. And these books should be read. But once in a while, a basic doctrine of our faith is explained or illustrated in a way that makes us feel like we are meeting an old friend for the first time; our friend is the same, but qualities we long took for granted are now recognized as rare and wonderful.

John Miller's latest book, *Come Back, Barbara*, breaks new ground by putting exciting new flesh on sturdy old bones. We all know that we should love our kids through thick and thin: love endures all things; don't give up; reject the sin but not the sinner. But parents who are contending with a rebellious child, particularly an older one in the late teens or early twenties, too often replace acceptance of the child and a legitimate burden for his or her well being with a pressuring insistence that the child conform so that parental pain is relieved. The story of Barbara Miller's flight from God and its effect on her parents is a tale of what it means to love someone who is breaking your heart.

John Miller and his daughter Barbara tell the agonizing story of her determination to make life work without God, telling enough details about her eight years of sinful living to let the reader feel both the stubborn emptiness in her soul and

9

how desperately God's Spirit was needed to help her parents learn to love her well. The power of the book is not in those details, but in the clear message that the grace of God provides a freedom and joy that, when tasted, are hard to resist. The book focuses on what it meant for John Miller to accept a daughter who rejected everything he had given his life to and how God used that love to draw Barbara to His perfect love.

Too many prodigal-son (or -daughter) stories have little of the realism of the biblical version, the horror of sin and the painful eagerness of a parent longing for the child's return. The Millers' narrative is no fluffy tale about parents who enjoy a quiet confidence as they pray easily for their naughty child. You can feel the struggle in Barbara's dad as he confronts his own sinfulness and lack of trust, worries about the toll of family turmoil on his wife, and wrestles with unloving anger, bitter heartache, and a deep sense of failure.

You can see the blindness of sin as Barbara recklessly moves from quiet rebellion to blatant immorality to respectable sinfulness, while oblivious to her parents' pain. And you can worship as you hear how God worked through a community who loved Barbara enough to prick her conscience and to bring her into the freedom and joy of forgiveness. The ending is happy, but it comes after years of the soul-searching that all true growth in love requires.

Two thoughts stand out as I read the book. One is the easily overlooked truth that forgiving others implies there is no excuse for what they have done. When we think about forgiving someone who has hurt us, it is natural to remind ourselves that "what that person did was really wrong! There's no excuse for it." That is precisely the point. If the offense could be reasonably explained, then the offender would need understanding, not forgiveness. In *Come Back, Barbara* the sins of both the father and the daughter are exposed without excuse. The effect is to provide a dark background against which the jewel of God's forgiving grace more brightly sparkles.

My second thought centers on the unique temptation that relational pain presents. When someone hurts us badly, our immediate impulse is to find relief. None of us likes pain. And the quickest way to feel a little better is to retreat from the one who hurt us; perhaps we pray from a safe distance or remind ourselves of their ingratitude. Resenting someone is more comfortable than feeling the hurtful impact of what they have done.

The pain of watching older children move in wrong directions, knowing that no word of rebuke or instruction will reach them, can be overwhelming. The work of God's grace in a parent's heart is most fully revealed when, after admitting their helplessness to bring about the change they deeply desire in their children, they persist in love.

There's more to love than we think. The implications of our Lord dying for us "while we were yet sinners" are staggering. Perhaps the great need of the church today is to face how badly we love and then to enter more fully into the costly grace of our forgiving Lord. Only then will we know the freedom to love others well, even when they grieve us deeply. *Come Back, Barbara* will convince you of the power of love, and more importantly, it will stir your soul to appreciate the message of God's grace with renewed wonder.

A Note from the Authors

The story is essentially told by C. John Miller, with Barbara Miller Juliani responding to each chapter with her account of events and her view of them. Each of us tried to tell the story as we felt it at the time, keeping hindsight to a minimum. It should be evident that we often had different views of the same incidents, but that is what the book is all about. The purpose is to show how a father and a daughter with conflicting values came to have a wonderful reconciliation through Christ's working changes in both of us.

A Father's Introduction

As we raised our five children, my wife and I believed that each was a gift from God, that all of them were special. We were convinced that God had given them to us for an important purpose, and as an expression of that faith, we made our children into our close friends. The story that follows is the journey we made with one of those friends, a friend who was even to forsake us for a time—our daughter Barbara. This is a story of intense sorrows, with us as parents being crushed many times by events beyond our control. But we always were Barbara's friends—no matter what she did; and for her part she always saw us as *her family*. Paradoxically this was true even when she bitterly rejected us and our values, and blamed us for her problems.

Now comes the hard question: If our home had such faith and love, did I fail Barbara as a father? If so, how? This book tells the full story. Although I do not believe that my child's flaws are always mine or are caused by me, I also know that I failed Barbara in ways too numerous to mention. I suspect every thinking parent knows that he or she blunders. But in my role as Barbara's father, there was a particular serious flaw that I now see, though I did not see it when she was an adolescent. It was a sin of omission more than of commission. In brief, my friendship with Barbara was inadequately cultivated when she entered the junior-high years. I did not

13

work to *touch* her inner life when she came to the crisis period that begins for most American youngsters upon entering the seventh or eighth grade. And I was blind to my failure.

But my tragic mistake is only the jumping-off point for the grand adventure that unfolds here. However inadequately I tell it, the events narrated in this book are beautiful in spite of their pain. Even before Barbara begins to change, you will see how I lose control of the situation and eventually lose my *need* to do so. Therein lies the divine paradox. I lose battle after battle. Some of it goes down hard. Repeatedly I get the stuffing kicked out of me in the conflict with my daughter. I did not like to live year after year with the tension of the battle and the constant feeling that things were completely out of my hands. But at the end of the story you discover that Barbara's change was not a fluke, a lucky turnabout. It came about because God was weaving a web of love around us all, and an important part of that web was his working through my being humbled.

At the end, I was as much a wayward father as Barbara was a wayward daughter. And of course, it was not my victory but my Father's. In his triumph I received back my daughter. She and I now walk together in sunshine after the storm that cleansed the air.

This book, then, is meant to encourage parents who may be walking in the shadows of failure. Some anxious parents with younger children are already anticipating failure, as they face the teen years with dread. They expect the worst. Other parents feel that the worst has already happened, seeing themselves battered and bruised by a rebellious adolescent.

The theme of the book is simply that if God could help someone like me—with all my sins and weaknesses—then he can help you and your family. Bringing up children is simpler than you or I ever thought. The master principle is simply this: Confront the conscience—and don't be impressed by outward conformity. But even if you have failed at this, the power of God's grace is so much stronger that you need never despair of your children, no matter what state they are in. This is as true of the nonconformist rebels as it is of the conformist rebels.

In this book you will also discover that God has a healing sense of humor. It makes me smile to think that he was seeking the rebellious father through the rebellious child. Obviously he wanted to change me right along with Barbara, and he worked at it by sending me a series of humbling defeats that lasted almost eight years. But the upside-down, queer thing is that the more I lost the more I won.

A Daughter's Introduction

I stood before my fellow students and nervously introduced the poem I was about to recite. "This is a poem," I said, "about a man who flees from God, but everywhere he turns he meets him. Finally he has no choice but to accept God's love for him." Then I recited Francis Thompson's "Hound of Heaven":

> I fled Him, down the nights and down the days;
> I fled Him, down the arches of the years;
> I fled Him, down the labyrinthine ways
> Of my own mind; and in the midst of tears
> I hid from Him, and under running laughter.

There I was, a skinny little eighth grader with no idea that I had just given a short summary of the next dozen years of my life. I hadn't even picked this poem; my father suggested it. I felt uncomfortable reciting it before my rowdy junior-high friends, but I never forgot the poem. Years later, after learning of God's love for me, I reread it with tears.

In those days I was a Christian—on the surface. I did all the right Christian things, like going to church and Christian school, but the reality—beneath the surface—was far different.

Sometimes reality broke through. For instance, during that year one of my teachers called my dad in for a conference. As

17

we sat in the small office, my teacher used words like "dishonest," "not working up to her potential," and "deceiving" to describe me. Afterward, when my dad asked me some questions about my honesty, I put him off with vague half-answers.

The reality was that I was a rebel in disguise. At eighteen I put off the disguise. It's a familiar story, one that has occurred many times in countless homes, for many people have had bad relationships with parents and have acted in destructive ways. There is nothing out of the ordinary in the bad judgment I showed in ordering my life. What makes this story stand out is that God used my parents to pursue me and to teach me about his love. Through their love, the Hound of Heaven was able to find me, and that is what makes this story worth telling.

Come Back, Barbara

Chapter One

"Come Back, Barbara"

*W*e are not a family of shouters. We don't raise our voices or even argue much, except in a joking way. And it certainly isn't our style to lose our tempers.

But this day was different. It was late July 1972. The place: Cuernavaca, a lovely paradisal city located on a high plateau about sixty miles south of Mexico City. The setting was a room on the second floor of Chula Vista, the gleaming white main building of the Alpha-Omega center for missionary outreach. It was midmorning. My eighteen-year-old daughter, Barbara, slender and darkly tanned, sat on a low single bed diagonally across from my chair. Near her on another chair was Rose Marie, her mother. Rose Marie is blue-eyed and blond, and at that moment her eyes were blazing.

"Mom, Dad," Barbara shouted, "I don't want your rules and morals. I don't want to act like a Christian anymore! And I'm not going to!"

"Barb," cried her mother, "stop it! Stop it right now!" Rose Marie left her chair and shook Barbara by the shoulders. "You're acting crazy! Listen to me! Do you know what you're doing?"

At that point I joined in with my own raised voice. It was

ineffectual. I felt stupid and embarrassed. Then we all began to weep, Barbara with anger and frustration, and Rose Marie and I out of anger and fear for our daughter.

The source of the tension had been Barbara's insistence that she had a right to "personal freedom" in her relationships with men. She was not giving an inch and neither were we. The next moment an angry Barbara bolted for the door and slammed it behind her with a defiant bang.

"Barbara Catherine," her mother called, "come back, come back!" The same words were in my own heart and on the tip of my tongue. But we might as well have saved our breath. Barbara was already downstairs, heading for the swimming pool shimmering in the subtropical sunlight. She had won the battle. We were stunned and felt like fools in our powerlessness.

Rose Marie looked pale in spite of her tan, and I was sick at heart. Everything seemed out of control. I felt that I had been the victim of invisible powers, like Oedipus hastening to his doom under the guidance of an iron, unfriendly fate. And I knew that I had somehow unwittingly contributed to my own defeat.

How had this crisis come about?

About a week before our son, Paul, had called us from our home in Jenkintown, Pennsylvania, to say that he was deeply concerned about Barbara. Since he was close to Barbara and knew her well, he felt that she had been spending too much time with some of her non-Christian friends and that they were having a harmful influence on her. He urged us to invite Barbara to Cuernavaca immediately. So after a phone call from us, Barbara agreed to fly down.

At first things appeared to stabilize. Juan, one of the fine young men working with Alpha-Omega, escorted her around Cuernavaca, unintentionally acting as her chaperone. But the bottom fell out the evening the three of us attended a Mexican wedding without Juan.

It was a magic night with the scent of a thousand flowers in the air. The fast beat of the mariachi music, the laughter, and the gaily dressed couples brought out Barbara's innermost longings. It quickly became clear that she couldn't wait to ally herself with some non-Christian man. The way she looked, the way she dressed, and the way she walked sent a clear message to the men around her: Barbara was ready to experiment with the world.

Soon a young man picked up the signals from the pretty señorita. As she sat at his table, I kept a fatherly eye on her, a thing that I did not like to do since our family had always operated on the basis of trust. Nothing particular troubled me, but I had the vague feeling that at the first opportunity she would jettison our family's moral values without a second thought. What so appalled me was that a "new Barbara" seemed to be emerging. What had happened to my friend and daughter? Inwardly I shuddered.

That evening was a terrific strain, even more for Rose Marie than for me. But what could we do?

We tried what most parents do. Early the next day, in that small hotel in Cuernavaca, we talked to Barbara and tried to reason with her. It didn't do much good. So Rose Marie and I went to our room and prayed. When we returned once more to talk with her, as I described at the beginning of this chapter, the whole scene went off like a bomb. Our words only made matters worse.

After Barbara slammed the door, we sat there in shock and confusion. We didn't say a word. We had always assumed that we had good communication with Barbara, based upon a shared faith. We had always thought of her as a Christian, at least since she had joined the church at the age of sixteen. But now, while we knew she was not acting like a Christian, we

23

still tried to treat her like one. Perhaps this was only a temporary lapse, we thought.

As parents, we were like two people working on a jigsaw puzzle who suddenly discover pieces in the box that do not seem to belong. It just didn't fit together. On the one hand, Barbara was acting like a pagan who couldn't wait to get out in the world "where the fun really is." On the other hand, we remembered her statement of faith when she became a full member of the church. She had spoken with seeming sincerity about Christ's having changed her life, and she had told us in a moving way what he meant to her.

Had she faked it? It just didn't seem possible. Her Christian life seemed to have been more than mere words. She had had a prominent part in helping a number of people become Christians. In doing so, she had certainly convinced them that she was a Christian. For instance, Jill Hebden, a high-school classmate now engaged to marry our son, Paul, had become a Christian largely through Barbara's example of Christian living among her peers in the local public high school.

Drugs had begun to enter the high school when Barbara was in the tenth grade, and Barbara had spoken out strongly against their use. In fact, her stand against drugs was so strong that it even prompted a school authority to call us and suggest that Barb was creating something of a myth about drugs in the school. In reflecting on Barbara's strength of character, Jill later said, "You certainly could've fooled me. I thought she was a Christian. She read her Bible regularly, and I know she turned down drugs."

So naturally we were taken aback by Barbara's claim that she was rejecting Christianity. But more importantly, we also thought she was implying that she had never been a Christian. It was muted but it was said. Still, we were not prepared to believe it.

In other ways, Cuernavaca was a high point in my life. I had prayed for an increase in my love for God, and although I became ill with dysentery not long after that prayer, still, during that sickness I came to experience God's love in a new way. The fruit of this new knowledge of him turned into a book that I wrote during that time. In a little over two weeks I wrote *Repentance and Twentieth Century Man*.

As I deepened in my experience of the joy of repentance, it just did not make sense that anyone would want to trade the fulfillment to be found in Christ for the short-term pleasures of the world. The whole thing just sounded crazy to Rose Marie and me, a nightmare that we hoped would vanish in the morning light.

Unfortunately, we were ten years too late to help Barbara. When our daughter was eight, we should have tried harder to face up to the truth about her inward life. But we could not help her now, not through persuasion and certainly not by our losing our tempers.

Barbara wanted freedom—freedom from all constraints, from parents, from church, from God. She was after the happiness that she sensed was to be found "out there," apart from home and Christianity, and she wanted to be happy *now*. To become happy she opted for the fast lane, determined to step on the gas and pay no attention to cautionary road signs. Like the younger son in the parable of the father's love, she wanted freedom from the parental home via a trip to the "far country."

Unfortunately, I was not like the father in the parable, nor were Rose Marie and I ready to let go of our child and entrust her to God. This unwillingness generated a lot of tension in our minds and made us slow to accept the idea that maybe Barbara had indeed faked many things during her adolescence. Who wants to admit to having been fooled by one's own child? But after Barbara slammed the door in Cuernavaca, we began to realize that it was too late, that she would have gone anyway, and that no one could have prevented her from "wasting her substance on riotous living."

25

In looking back on that morning, Rose Marie later said, "When Barb announced that she was 'not a Christian and didn't want to be one,' my world came crashing in on me. I reacted with anger and fear. I simply couldn't handle it. My own barriers were too high for me to be able to open up and deal calmly with what she was saying. I felt humiliated and betrayed."

Later that day, when all of us cooled down, our family's habitual dislike of conflict reasserted itself. Rose Marie and I sought out Barbara and invited her to come with us and her younger sister, Keren, on an expedition to the center of Cuernavaca. Beneath the surface the conflict was still there, but we managed to treat each other almost normally as we walked the half mile to the city center.

There we seated ourselves for lunch at an outdoor café. Our sense of humor even returned, at least momentarily. A young boy, probably around nine or ten, saw us. As he headed toward us he quickly transformed himself from a healthy youngster into a beggar with a twisted arm and leg. It was great acting. If I had not seen this little faker walking normally just a moment before, I would have been fooled, but I had seen him walking along the sidewalk and happily talking to his companions, and so had the whole family. So we greeted his performance with applause—but no money. He grinned sheepishly and departed.

Looking back, I can see that his game had in it a certain appropriate symbolism. Do we not all have our little games we play on one another and even on ourselves to get what we want? In our family relationships, don't we often transform ourselves into cripples to get our own way? At that time I sensed that maybe a game was being played in our family, but I was too emotionally drained to learn the rules.

On a profounder level I also sensed that our family was under attack. Dark powers seemed to be ranged against us. As much as I loved subtropical Cuernavaca—with its sharp, clear air in the morning, its brilliant radiance at noon, and its evenings suffused with soft air—all that now seemed secondary. I felt the tread of evil walking the earth, laying traps for my feet, and whispering words of despair to my heart: "Give up on Barb, that ungrateful child." But I refused to accept her renunciation of Christ as the conclusive victory of Satan over Christ in her life. I felt I ought to give up, to reject her the way she was rejecting us, but vaguely I felt this would be to play her game. So inwardly I determined to wait on God, to lean on him in the midst of my fears and sense of defeat, and indeed I found a measure of release in this preliminary surrender of the situation to him. I could not call it full peace, but it had in it the beginnings of a quiet acceptance of his will for Barbara.

As we flew home to Philadelphia in August, we were aware that Barbara was still alienated from us, though outwardly she was civil. As we went through customs in Atlanta, I was still wrestling. My hope was that Barbara, in spite of herself, was still a Christian, that she was simply going through a time of temporary backsliding. But I also suspected that that was my own little game, my own private fable that Barbara had never deceived us about being a Christian. What made it so hard was that I had been deceived by a good friend—not just a daughter. I felt betrayed.

At home in Jenkintown, Barb was eager to get out of the house and spend her time with those friends who had become her new models of conduct, in fact, the very friends that Paul had been concerned about before. Barbara didn't even seem to take seriously her preparations for her first year at Dickinson College. Rose Marie was upset by Barbara's new pattern of escape. Rose Marie needed Barbara to help her with the care and cleaning of our large house with its thirteen rooms. Rose Marie, weakened by major surgery that had taken place not long before our sojourn in Mexico, felt abandoned. As she said later, "I felt Barbara should stay home and get things in order for school, and I told her so. My saying it to her didn't help things. I guess this was the last time I had any conflict with her—there were hurts that went deep—and I don't believe I was open enough at that time to help her with her hurts."

As I sorted through my thoughts that August, I came to more definite answers to the questions that had haunted me. One question that would not go away was this: Why had I let myself be so completely deceived by Barbara? The answer, I thought, was that family pride had blinded me to what she was really like.

More than once when she was growing up I had caught Barbara in deceptions. For instance, there was the time when Barbara was eight and was caught lying about brushing her teeth. At the time we lived in Redwood City, California. To help organize our family responsibilities while I did research on my Ph.D., I made up a hygiene-and-duty chart for the family. Every day each of our four older children was expected to check off the tasks completed. Barbara's chart showed that she had faithfully brushed her teeth every day during the past week. But one day Paul and Ruth presented Barbara's toothbrush to Rose Marie and me. It was as dry as a bone. Acting as self-appointed enforcers, they had been examining her toothbrush for almost a week, and though she had checked the chart, the truth was that she had not brushed her teeth for a long time. What was even worse, Barbara, in spite of persuasion and discipline, would not admit that she had lied. She proved to be extremely stubborn. It was a powerful indicator of something wrong in her inner life, and it was also a call for us as parents to reexamine our approach.

But the truth is that we cooperated with our own deception. We failed to look the unpleasant truth squarely in the eye and do something about it. Most of the time Barbara conformed outwardly to the standards of the family, and we were too easily satisfied with that. We avoided the conflict that would have occurred if we had asked Barbara more probing questions about her values and motivations, what you might call her real wants. In fact, by accepting her superficial performance, we kept her from seeing what her real heart hungers were.

Facing up to this was unpleasant for me. But it was also healing. There were plenty of mysteries in the whole situation and to some extent there still are. But these were tangible truths that I could use in changing my own life. I sensed I needed to humble myself and acknowledge my failure as a parent. This helped clear my mind, and this acceptance led to a new release. I did not want to be emotionally crippled by my failures. Once I had identified them I asked God's forgiveness, and knowing I was forgiven renewed my confidence that he was present and working in our situation.

I cannot stress enough the importance of honest confession for parents who carry a burden of repressed guilt. There is nothing worse than wallowing in failure and enjoying the self-torture generated by it. In that state I am no help to anyone— not even myself. In fact, I am like the Mexican boy, pretending to be a cripple.

So it was not destructive to find out something of my weakness in bringing up Barbara, to admit the wrong and find God's pardon. Released from that burden through repent-ance, I was, with God's help, able to accept more of the truth about Barbara and to deal with her more honestly. This truth hurt, but it was like the pain of childbirth. I had to accept that our hard work and love had failed in Barbara's case. She was not just our "dear Barbara, with the tender heart," but a first-rate operator, a talented counterfeiter. But she too was being unveiled. Coming to the surface at last were her pugnacity toward us and her determination to turn her life into a disaster.

It was ghastly but it was the truth, and we needed to face the truth. There is no worse evil than to deny evil, to pretend that it is not there. I am not ignorant of human depravity, but I had long denied that it could exist in our family. We are orderly, hard-working people; our home is a place where we feel understood and affirmed. We paid our dues for all of this by succeeding in life. Our unspoken motto was: "Work hard and success will follow."

What we failed to account for was that outward conformity to an orderly family life proves nothing. A child can put on all the external forms of Christian life and good order, and not be near God at all. For the parent to fail to look below the surface and to pass lightly over inner motivations is often to let the child put a veneer over life. The inward person is left untouched, and when that happens the inward self can easily become hardened and embittered.

As parents, our grief during this time was intense. We had lost the battle and knew the humiliations of exposure and defeat. But from our present vantage point we can see how it was also entirely under the perfect plan of God, the beauty of which we were not able to see at that time. Then it was like walking through a dark forest on an invisible trail. We could see nothing of what lay ahead, but we made our way along the path with fear and trembling. Yet because our hands were held securely in the hand of our heavenly Father, we could trust the way to his eyes.

But even then we felt God had a purpose in it all, as he stripped away our façade of self-sufficiency. We had placed great confidence in Christian nurture in the home and in Christian private schools. But no one grows into grace through a Christianized environment. No one gets to God by moral self-improvement. You only get to God by being transplanted from your natural soil into the life of Christ by a personal faith in him. In our nurture of Barbara we had unconsciously forgotten these foundational truths.

We were also beginning to learn that we were entirely dependent on God to change Barbara and that eventually he would renew her heart and life. Rose Marie put it even more personally: "At that time I was in danger of complete despair. What kept me from giving up was the knowledge that Barbara did belong to God and that in his own time and way he would bring her back."

We were slowly learning what Paul so eloquently expresses in 2 Corinthians 1:8–10: "We were under great pressure, far beyond our ability to endure, so that we despaired even of life. Indeed, in our hearts we felt the sentence of death. But this happened that we might not rely on ourselves but on God, who raises the dead. He has delivered us from such a deadly peril, and he will deliver us."

Barbara's Response

*A*ctually, nobody in our family is a shouter—except me. The summer I graduated from high school I did a lot of shouting. Mostly I worked on getting my own way and staying as far away from my family as possible. Even when I flew to Mexico to join my parents, I was still determined to be as separate as possible from them and their lifestyle.

My first opportunity came at the wedding we were invited to at a luxurious country club in Cuernavaca. The setting was beautiful, the band was good, and there were quite a few young men eager to dance with me. I was flattered by the attention. I danced, strolled in the moonlight, and finally ended up eating at another table with a young medical student. I could tell that my parents didn't approve, but I was having fun and was too embarrassed to tell my new friend that my parents wouldn't allow me to dance or sit with him. As we communicated in stumbling Spanish and English I used up my stock phrases to tell him that I had a sister and I gave him the name of our hotel.

I left the wedding happy to have been able to flirt but sure that I would never see the medical student again. Imagine my surprise when my "paramour" showed up at the hotel the next day with a friend who wanted to double date my sister! I informed them in broken Spanish that my sister was twelve and that they had to leave immediately before my parents saw them. They left, and I breathed a sigh of relief.

By the time my parents sat me down to talk about my conduct at the wedding, I was feeling pretty self-righteous. I thought of the whole thing as a harmless flirtation, and when the guys had shown up at the hotel I had quickly packed them off. During the discussion with my parents I was in the enviable position of being able to say (again and again in injured tones), "But I only did . . ." My argument was that I had done nothing wrong and that they were overreacting. In a sense this was true—they did overreact to the situation. But at the same time, they had begun to read my spirit correctly. Before, I had always taken pains to conceal anything about myself that I knew my parents wouldn't approve of. But now I was sick of being a hypocrite, and my true self was emerging. That is what actually upset them.

That time in Mexico was one of the most painful experiences of my life. It was even hard for me to read my father's account of it. I can still see the three of us sitting on the balcony of their hotel room. The warmth of the sun, the bright pink of the azaleas, and the green of the trees shading us were all lost on me. I was spending my time measuring the distance between the balcony and the ground, and wondering if I could possibly jump safely to the lawn below.

What made this confrontation particularly painful was that when my parents started to understand what I was really like, they reacted with fear and anger. I had long concealed my real desires because I did not want to risk their disapproval and the loss of their good opinion. Now my worst fears were being realized. I felt helpless. I did not want to live the way they wanted me to, and in fact, I could not. While I had made resolutions to act like a Christian at various times in my life, I always ended up frustrated by my failures. I thought that my only option was to just accept myself for who I was and hope that my parents would too. My parents did not know it, but they were asking me to do the impossible—to be a Christian when I wasn't. And I had no way of becoming what they wanted me to be. All of my hopes and desires were taking me in the completely opposite direction.

In Mexico I decided that being myself meant distancing myself from my family. It seemed too painful to be around each other—painful for me and, I was aware, painful for them.

Chapter Two

The Devastating Blow

*I*t was to be an unforgettable day. In early September we drove Barbara from our home near Philadelphia to Dickinson College, located in the central Pennsylvania town of Carlisle. I was behind the wheel, Rose Marie was next to me, and Barbara was in the back.

Little was said. The personal coolness among the three of us made me appreciate the beauty of the late summer. Often in central Pennsylvania, the summer sky is covered by a milky haze, a muggy condition that can continue well into September. But on that day the blue sky looked like it had been newly painted. The sun was shining with pleasant warmth.

Under Barbara's guidance we found our way through the tree-lined streets of Carlisle to her freshman dormitory. "This is my dorm," she said with her first sign of enthusiasm of the day. I suspected that beneath it all she was nervous and anxious.

After I deposited her suitcases in the entrance of the colonial-style building, a dignified lady informed me that we were in the right place. "But," she added with authority, "freshmen girls cannot occupy their rooms till five o'clock."

After a plea from me she agreed to allow the suitcases to be deposited in Barbara's room until five. The law had spoken but had also relented slightly.

While the luggage was being taken to the room, Rose Marie and I introduced ourselves to a distinguished-looking couple who had just come into the entranceway. They were accompanied by their tall, blond daughter. Everyone was a little self-conscious. Like our daughter, the blond girl was trying to look self-assured and adult.

After some small talk we excused ourselves, and the three of us went for a drive. We finally ended up on a road that led into a parklike area not far from Carlisle. The dirt road paralleled a quiet stream, shaded by ancient maples and oaks, and decorated here and there by dogwood. Through openings in the trees the afternoon sun poured into the forest and formed bright pools of golden light on the roadway, the leaves, and the surface of the creek.

I stopped the car for a few minutes to appreciate the beauty all around me. I am an Oregonian by origin, and Oregonians are viewers. Part of our state's snobbery is that we pride ourselves on being seers, unlike Californians whom we imagine to be activistic doers who do not take time to appreciate the natural world. On that day, I stepped out of our car and walked down by the creek and then back up among the large maples. I tossed a few stones in the creek. It was a grand world!

For me, God's creation is a continual reminder to keep human problems in perspective, and I encourage others to do the same. But that day nobody was listening. The old times were gone. No one wanted to hear about the loveliness of light upon dark or listen to the sound of the stream. So much for nature, so much for sentiment. Rose Marie and Barbara no doubt thought I was being a Pollyanna. I probably was. For although I knew there were some deep tensions, I did not see how close to the surface they actually were.

Before she left for college, Barbara's relationships with her friends had led to increasing conflict between Rose Marie and her. I didn't help matters by visiting one of her friends and pointing out gently but clearly that this person's hedonism was pulling Barbara into a destructive way of life. Neither my effort nor Rose Marie's produced anything but more resentment and self-pity in Barbara, who now felt outraged by our "persecution."

The situation was ghastly. From the vantage point of the present, I know it would have been wiser for Rose Marie and me to have kept our concerns to ourselves. But at the time we still had at least a faint hope that Barbara had only slipped into a temporary phase and that the shadows would soon lift from her life. We felt that if anything could be done to protect her from self-destruction, we should do it.

On that first day at college, Barbara was intent on sending us a loud message, so determined was she to cut the cords of love that bound us together. It came as we drove back to Carlisle and parked in front of her dorm. I don't even remember what was said. Possibly one of us said something to enflame her, but at any rate she stepped out of the car, slammed the door, and walked quickly into the dorm without saying good-bye.

I was stunned, brokenhearted, and ashamed. I sensed something that I had never felt from Barbara before. It was no one thing she did, not even slamming the door, but rather the whole subtle message that she was ashamed of us and our Christianity. Her intonations, her coldness of manner, her superior look—all these things made me aware that she was telling us, "Hands off. I don't like your style of life, and I don't want to be around you."

This leave taking was much harder to handle than the slammed door in Cuernavaca. On our way home to Jenkintown, Rose Marie and I agreed that we had been hit a devastating blow. Our five children—Roseann, Ruth, Paul, Barbara, and Keren—were born in that order. As the youngest of the first four and older than Keren by five years, Barb had been part of an intensely loyal family group. Now Rose Marie and I felt we were experiencing an amputation, a violent cutting away of part of our flesh. And the severing had not been a clean one—though it certainly was complete.

I was angry and ashamed. For the first time I was prepared to admit that I was wounded. My feelings cried out, "Ingrate! You don't want anything to do with us! Well, why should I want anything to do with you?"

It was a good question: Why should I have anything more to do with Barbara? It would have been entirely natural for me to reject her or hold a grudge or lapse into self-pity. In the months that followed, Barbara made it increasingly clear that she was locking the door between her life and ours, and throwing away the key. She acquired a non-Christian boyfriend who was clearly out of sympathy with our values, and Barbara finally told us plainly that she had made a phony public profession of faith at Mechanicsville Chapel. She had never been a Christian. She resigned her membership in the church and announced that she was at last a happy and fulfilled person.

In my numbness I wondered what I should be learning from God. I knew that I could not reject Barbara, and the temptation to do so faded pretty quickly. But what *was* I supposed to do now? On one level, there wasn't much I could do. I doubted if a phone call would be welcome.

But one idea did occur to me, an idea that forced me into some healthy self-examination. It was simply this: Did I love Barbara as she really was—or did I only love my idea of Barbara? I knew from my own counseling that family members often don't love each other for who they really are. They love the ideal they have created of the other person. Love from God, I knew, is tougher and clearer-eyed. It loves people as they really are. God's love can be honest about people while holding on to them until that love changes them.

I gradually understood that it was this kind of honest love that I needed. After so much mutual battering, it was not immediately clear how to achieve that kind of love, but it was a great step forward to see that this was what I needed. And I knew that God would give it to me if I really sought it.

During the next few months Rose Marie and I began to take our first tottering steps in exercising this kind of Christlike love, love that is able to look through the hard outer shell and see the desperately needy person inside. To better practice this kind of unconditional love, we did three things:

1. We accepted Barbara's new self-identification. She was a non-Christian and should be accepted as such. To do otherwise would be to suppress the truth and hinder any renewed interest in the Christian faith.

2. We apologized to her for having done too much parenting of the wrong sort. Barbara reported to us that she had had five parents while growing up—Dad, Mom, Rose-ann, Ruth, and Paul. All of us apologized for our nagging and patronizing attitudes toward her. She seemed to accept the apologies.

3. We made no further attempt to regulate or control her behavior. We specifically decided not to comment again on her choice of friends. This last decision especially took much grace, which could only be received through prayer.

What had we done exactly? I think it can be put this way: we were not just giving up control of Barbara's life; we were also recognizing that we had to give up our efforts to exercise *influence* over her basic choices. That is where it really hurts for the caring parent to pull back, and the struggle to do so can be intense. Why? Because every parent worthy of the name is absolutely convinced that he or she knows better than the child how to run the child's life. But the pressure of this conviction often oppresses or confuses the young person. At a certain point, in spite of wrong and rebellious attitudes, a young adult rightly senses that he or she must begin to make decisions personally. A parent's attempts to exercise influence over the life of the grown child simply hinder the child's coming to maturity through exposure to the blows of life lived outside the parental nest.

For the morally sensitive parent, this can be a kind of death sentence. The parent can actually end up hating the child or being consumed by fear of "all the things that can happen" to a naïve young person. But for Christians like Rose Marie and me this kind of death had in it a hidden resurrection. For that is the way the Christian faith works. It has in it a death side and a resurrection side. It was a death to our dreams when Barbara identified herself as a non-Christian; it was another death to admit that she had received too much parenting from Rose Marie, the three older children, and me; and it was the ultimate death to recognize that we no longer could or should try to influence her choices.

But with that sentence of death, we were gradually being set free to know God as the "God who raises the dead" (2 Corinthians 1:9). In the next chapter, this resurrection began to take place.

Barbara's Response

*W*ith both relief and fear I greeted my small, sterile-looking dorm room at Dickinson College. My resolution in Mexico to distance myself from my family and the Christian community was easier said than done. Back at home, my mother and I had constantly bickered over trivial issues, but underlying these was a deep rift in our relationship. I kept attempting to pull away and they kept trying to stop me. I looked forward to college as an end of their control and thus a cessation of hostilities. I was also petrified at the prospect of having to make new friends. I was afraid that no one would like me, and I was determined that I wasn't going to be hampered by any ties to Christianity.

I was not aware that my dad felt rejected by my obvious desire to get rid of him and Mom as quickly as possible. I had spent a lot of time with my parents in new social situations, and I knew that at any minute my father might begin witnessing to one of my roommates. I felt that neither the wealthy Jewish girl from New York (I was awed by her closet crammed full of new clothes from her father's store) nor the quiet, well-bred ("I have a boyfriend at Princeton") Southern girl were going to feel comfortable when my dad started giving his testimony. I knew I would be mortified. So I hustled them out with never a thought for how I might be making them feel.

With my parents gone, I quickly went to work gathering a new group of friends. Freshman girls at Dickinson experience a rush of attention from the upperclassmen, and I was no exception. I remember often setting up three dates for one evening. I would go to dinner with one young man, to a party with another, and then take a late night walk with still another. I smoked marijuana and drank regularly through the week. Most of the time I went to bed so late that I had difficulty getting up in the morning to work in the cafeteria. Many mornings my friends would laugh as I served scrambled eggs while still dozing.

Schoolwork was not my highest priority. I would often meet my best friend, Sally, before my 10:00 A.M. class for coffee and donuts. Invariably, one of us would suggest cutting class and tooling around in her little orange MG. The other, after a little arm twisting, would agree, and we would be off roaming through the streets of Carlisle or driving at high speeds through the beautiful countryside.

Still, although I seemed not to have a care in the world, there were flies in the ointment. The lies and deceptions that I thought I left behind in Philadelphia turned out to be a pretty basic part of my personality. I lied to my new friends to make myself seem more experienced and "cool" than I really was. My conscience, which I was trying to ignore, would surface at the worst moments. Once I was at a sleep-over party at the home of someone's conveniently absent parents. We all got high and lay on the Oriental rug in the huge living room, laughing and being silly. But later that night I experienced intense fear and began to cry for my father. I spent most of the night sitting in my bed and shaking. In the morning I dismissed it as a bad reaction to the marijuana. I wanted nothing to intrude on my scenario of what happy people did. Anything that contradicted this I simply shoved out of my mind. I was determined to prove to myself and my parents that my decision to leave Christianity had made me happy.

42

Although I couldn't acknowledge it, there was an irony to my life at that time. I was no longer an unhappy non-Christian pretending to be a happy Christian. Now I was pretending to be happy while underneath I had all of the same fears and insecurities that I had struggled with all of my life. In effect, I had merely exchanged one set of lies for another.

Chapter Three

Endurance Through Prayer

*F*or most of September and October we had little contact with Barbara. Rose Marie asked many people to pray for her and us—prayers that were greatly needed as Barbara worked out the implications for her new independence. Only God enabled us to bear up under the weight of unfolding events. Our whole relationship with Barbara was an endless war game, with Rose Marie and I cast in the role of losers.

In late October, for example, we learned that Barbara had come to Philadelphia a number of times, but had neither visited us or phoned. That hurt.

Rose Marie especially felt it was a personal rejection of her love. She had always loved all our children in a special way, and she had often reached out to Barbara as a caring mother helping a struggling child. When Barbara was only one year old, Rose Marie had faithfully applied splints to Barbara's crooked legs and helped her bear the discomfort of wearing it during those hot California days. Rose Marie had rescued the overly ambitious three-year-old from the swift waters of the Smith River in northern California. During Barbara's first year in school, Rose Marie had helped the struggling defeatist learn to read. Rose Marie had patiently borne the undisci-

45

plined habits of Barbara's teenage years, always ready to listen to her problems. Rose Marie had developed a close bond with Barbara through caring for her during a severe case of dysentery, through camping trips in California and Oregon, and through a happy summer Barbara spent with us in Spain. "Her rejection was beyond me," said Rose Marie. "I went numb."

The next blow came when Barbara moved in with her boyfriend, Tom Morris. After he wrote us to say that he was now living with our daughter, I made a trip to Dickinson where I presented to Barbara and Tom the case for sex within the bounds of marriage. I don't remember much about the conversation, but I know I failed to convince them that sensualism eventually carries its own revenges.

Although Rose Marie and I were still taking it on the chin, I knew by Thanksgiving that prayer was beginning to change us. We were responding to Barbara more as adult Christians and less as touchy parents. We were making progress in overcoming our need to exercise control over Barbara. Even when I went over to Dickinson, I was relatively free from the compulsion to act as schoolmaster straightening out an erring pupil.

I began to approach Barbara as a non-Christian needing help instead of as an offending daughter—which is no small victory for a parent in pain. Not that there wasn't distress in my heart, but I was learning to endure it because people were praying for her and for us. From that time forward, Rose Marie and I began to talk less about the problem and to pray more—not just for Barbara but also for the new church in Jenkintown that was beginning to meet in our home.

In November, Rose Marie and I organized a weekly prayer meeting in our home. We met on Wednesday evenings for at least two hours. Our intention was to seek God's wisdom in discerning whether he wanted us to begin a new church in our area. We asked him to reveal his will by showing us "a token for good." We wanted to see God bring about conversions and raise up church leaders as a confirmation that it was his work alone that would establish such a church. The prayer meetings centered on praise and claiming the promises of God. Through the study of Scripture I came to the view that truly biblical corporate prayer must focus on two things: (1) praise for the greatness of Christ's work on the cross and his resurrection and (2) claiming Jesus' promise to send the Spirit to revive us as we pray with one mind for his presence (Luke 11:13; Acts 1:13–14).

During the first month rarely more than eight people attended. By the end of three months, in January 1973, two of the people who said they were not believers had made commitments to Christ, and by that time nearly twenty-five people were attending.

Soon the Wednesday-evening prayer time became known as a victory hour where Christ was working in unusual ways. More and more prayers were being answered, and the evening was dominated by praise for the Father. Soon there were more professions of faith and radical renewals in the lives of a number of longtime believers.

During this period, a renewed hope for Barbara's eventual turn to Christ was born in Rose Marie and me. Put yourself in our position. We were still confused. Since our daughter had worn all the badges of the Christian faith and had thrown them away, we inevitably wondered: Is she an apostate who has renounced Christ? Is she beyond the help of our prayers? After all, if anyone knew about the inner workings of the Christian faith, Barb should. Was this, then, a fall from grace that had no hope of repentance? These questions were in our minds. But as we waited on God in prayer, solid and helpful answers began to come.

Soon Wendell "Bud" Haberen, one of the elders at Mechanicsville Chapel, where I had been pastor until the beginning of 1972, met with Barbara and heard her story. As a good friend of Barbara's, he heard her out and asked her some searching questions. Afterward he said to us, in effect, "I believe her. I don't see her as some kind of hopeless case, without any possibility of coming to God. She is just a non-Christian who has become honest. She is a non-Christian acting like a non-Christian. Personally I don't see how she could have ever become a real Christian without admitting she wasn't one first."

There was hope in his insight. He explained that Christian parents sometimes put too much weight on a child's having a conversion experience. His point was that "a commitment to Christ," if it is not followed by a changed life, might be a religious experience, but it is not a genuine conversion. In his view it is a form of self-deception to treat your child as a backslidden Christian or a hopeless apostate if the young person has never shown the fruit of a changed life. He noted with a smile, "I'm an example of what I'm saying. Don't forget that you led me to Christ *after* I had a 'conversion experience.'"

Rose Marie said later of this counsel: "It came to me as an unbelievable relief. I was confused. I was afraid that Barbara was an apostate, someone to be excommunicated by the church and then forgotten as a hopeless reprobate. But the idea that she was simply a non-Christian faking it meant that she could become a Christian eventually, maybe even soon. My mind was clearing up fast, and I was free to pray for her in faith. From that point on I did not doubt that God was finally going to save her no matter what she did."

Many times we parents fail right here, by not taking the *time* to wait upon the Lord in prayer, to ask with confident faith for his wisdom in our understanding of how to relate to our children. But when we earnestly and sincerely claim the transforming wisdom of the Spirit, what we learn is surprising. We ask for the transforming presence of the Spirit from the Father as promised by Jesus in Luke 11:1–13. Then when he visits us he reveals that it has been very wrong to give way to despair. Despair of God's help for the child is unbelief, the gravest of sins.

Such pessimism often leads parents into a second mistake, one that the Spirit is eager to overcome. It is simply that in our doubts and anxieties we give God little opportunity to be God over the situation. We read books, seek out counselors, and talk endlessly about "our problem." We are so eager to find the "magic bullet" that will cure all our disease and to do anything to bring about an immediate recovery of the prodigal and free us from our pain that we fail to see that we too are far from God. Stated positively, the Father wants to bring us as parents back to the intimate fellowship of his house. He is so very wise! He knows it is silly of us to try to bring our children to the Father's home when we ourselves are not living in its joy and warmth. So his method is to bring us near to his own heart and experience his peace. Then by our changed lives we begin to magnetize the child to return to the abundance of the Father's house.

The Spirit's aim is to overcome our restless human wisdom and hasty actions. His supreme concern is for us to get to know the Father well and wait on him in prayer for wisdom to learn how to touch the inner life of the many Barbaras in our lives.

We would never have learned this crucial lesson if the Father had not given us grace to pray and ask others for their prayers. Through those prayers we were learning a new perspective. We had a desperate need to see Barbara through God's compassionate eyes. Now, mysteriously we lost any bitterness in our hearts toward her. It simply disappeared. We no longer even talked much about the problem of Barbara. As the events of the summer and the early fall began to fade from our memories, we simply loved Barbara and that was enough.

By Christmas, Tom and Barbara were as warmly welcomed to our home as any of the other members of our family. I had a special love in my heart for both of them, a love that I believe was natural, neither fawning nor overbearing, but accepting. From the bottom of my heart I forgave Barbara, and I did the same for Tom. That act of forgiveness released the love of God in my life to work as a divine power. I found myself forgiving them on an ongoing basis for anything that grieved me in their lives and constantly replacing any bitterness with Christ's love. Forgiveness and love became a whole new lifestyle for me.

It's ironic, but the Lord had used my inability to forgive and love Barbara and Tom to drive me to him in total need. It was my midnight hour and I was the man who had no bread (Luke 11:5–8). In the Middle East it is a shame to have no bread for a guest, and here I was the man who was weak and ashamed. That's how I learned to beg in prayer. When I did pray this way, I discovered that as you seek and keep seeking you receive more bread than you can eat. The Father supplies the bread of the Spirit, and he does so abundantly. That bread consisted of a new wisdom, compassion, and a bit of desperately needed humility. In a word, revival had begun in my life, and its effects were to be seen in the brokenness and repentance that has so often characterized New Life Presbyterian Church, the congregation that emerged from the Wednesday-night meetings during those dark days.

Obviously the Son of God had worked in Rose Marie's and my hearts to keep us from missing the opportunity of a lifetime—to be like him in our thinking about Barbara and our seeking of her. I can never thank God enough for the way he turned a seamy, humbling, and painful experience into a grand adventure crowned with his love.

I realize that some hurting parents may think that I make loving a rebellious son or daughter sound easy. It may even be thought that Rose Marie and I were on a higher plane of spirituality than the more garden-variety suffering Christians who have family members living in rebellion to God. After all, if enduring, persevering prayer gives you that kind of speedy release from tensions, then maybe you are, in spite of what you said, offering us "a magic bullet."

But I don't view learning to wait on God as an easy thing to do at all. There were plenty of frustrations. Barbara was, in fact, sliding downhill throughout this period in her life and did not seem at all touched by our prayers. But at this stage of the relationship the one needing change was not her but her father. And that happened as I made a more total commitment to prayer as the power for forgiveness as a prevailing lifestyle. As forgiveness controlled my attitudes, I was able to love Barbara through thick and thin. Whenever I discovered myself angry or frustrated over her behavior, I simply forgave her all over again and saw the Spirit of love again ruling in my attitude toward her and her friends.

So my counsel for hurting parents is to learn to wait on God in prayer. Mobilize others to pray for you and your rebellious child. But give your prayers God's focus. Study Luke 11:1–13 about the promise of the Spirit, and soak yourself in the parable of the father's love in Luke 15:11–32. It will help you learn your need to endure, to wait, to keep your mouth shut, and to forgive and love. Persevere in it all. You will leave your bitterness and anger behind as you set forth on the grandest adventure of your life.

Barbara's Response

*W*hile the surface Barbara continued to put on a happy face, the frightened and insecure Barbara was desperately looking for someone to provide her with confidence and security. I found that someone in Tom Morris. Handsome, athletic, smart, he had all of the attributes that I considered important. But even more attractive to me was his willingness to step in where my father left off and take charge of my life. He counseled me to go to my classes, eat right, and get to bed on time. If I hadn't met him, I would probably have collapsed from nervous exhaustion and ended up in the hospital.

Within a few weeks of meeting, we were spending all our time together and I was staying overnight in his dorm room. He came to visit my family when I went home for Christmas and his take-charge attitude made a good impression, especially on my mother. When he arrived, we were all getting ready for my brother's wedding, and the house needed to be cleaned for the rehearsal dinner that my parents were hosting. Tom walked in on the midst of this confusion and immediately offered to vacuum the house. My mom gratefully accepted, and their relationship was off on the right foot. Later when we were opening Christmas presents and all of the Christmas paper caught fire, it was Tom who stomped it out. His specialty was bringing order to confusion and chaos, and in my gratitude I did not notice that I had exchanged one father for another.

My parents' good opinion of Tom was strained by our decision to live together in Carlisle over the summer. This was more my doing than Tom's. I could not stand the thought of going back to live with my parents for a whole summer without my new protector. So we wrote my dad to tell him our plans. Dad called and immediately came to see us. I remember eating lunch with him in a small dark diner on the main road through Carlisle. As huge trucks barreled past us, I picked at my food and attempted to explain to my father why I was doing what I was. Since I myself did not really know, it was a tough session. One thing my father said made a big impression on me. When he found out that Tom and I had been living together at school and were simply continuing this pattern for the summer, his comment was, "Since God is a God of truth, then I have to be happy that I know the truth and I am not still believing a lie about you."

My mother's reaction was not so easy to bear. Although she said nothing to me, my dad mentioned that she had become quite ill in the last couple of days. Since I knew that sickness was my mother's response to stress, I also knew that the person to blame for her illness was me. Even though I realized that I was causing my parents pain, I still continued with my plans. The thought of being with them and experiencing their disappointment was still too much. I didn't think they could love me the way I was and I preferred to stay with someone who seemed to love me for myself. So instead of coming home to a large, beautiful home in the suburbs of Philadelphia, I chose to live in a small, hot apartment in Carlisle, while toiling at the local cleaners for $1.75 an hour. Tom went to summer school while I worked, and we settled into a relationship that resembled that of an old married couple.

Chapter Four

The Marriage Game

Will you have this man to be your lawfully wedded husband?"

"I will."

With those words Barbara's boyfriend, Tom, became her husband. The date was January 5, 1974. The whole occasion was carried off with style. Even nature cooperated. The day before, an inch of snow had dusted the stones of the Episcopal church and its lovely grounds with silver. It made the black of the leafless tree branches stand out starkly against the white snow. A romantic person might have felt transported to an old English village.

Barbara never looked prettier than in her white wedding dress, and broad-shouldered Tom was handsome in his dark suit. I modified the service so that distinctly Christian elements were removed, since neither they nor I wanted them to be taking specifically Christian vows. But as they expected, I preached a short message about Christ's redeeming love and with so much joy that a number of their college friends were moved to talk with me about it afterward.

One of them said to me, in essence, "I felt held by what you said. It was as though maybe there was something really important and mysterious in life that I had missed, something you knew about and I didn't."

As I talked with a number of them and shared my joy in knowing Christ, I had a premonition of good things to come. I was convinced that some of these young people would one day become Christians.

This was the only wedding of any of our five children in which none of the others had a part in the ceremony. Not that there was friction; it just did not seem fitting to mix the Christians with the wedding party. Barbara felt it, and so did her brother and three sisters. Except for Roseann, Barbara's oldest sister who was with her husband, Jim, in Japan, the others all pitched in and helped in various ways. So did longtime Christian friends from Mechanicsville Chapel, our newly organized New Life Presbyterian Church, and West-minster Theological Seminary.

Barbara's older sister Ruth, blond, blue-eyed, impish, full of fun and seriousness all at once, made Barbara's wedding dress, fixed curtains for their apartment in Carlisle, and joined Rose Marie and Keren, our youngest, in cleaning up the couple's home. Another person who gave the wedding his all, out of love for Barbara and our family, was a former Black Muslim whom Barbara had a part in bringing to Christ. A talented cook, he catered the wedding in nearly royal style, assisted by a dozen Christian women who volunteered to help. He prepared a splendid smorgasbord and arranged it with an artist's touch.

It was a wonderful outpouring of love. I think even Barbara was moved. The caterer, with a big smile, said to her gently, "Barb, I don't understand all that has happened to you. But you can't keep running away from the love of Jesus forever. One day he's going to catch up with you."

My hope was that Barb would change. Would not marriage open a new and healing chapter in Barbara's life? Sadly, I soon knew that she was still on the run from God. With her values and Tom's, there was not much chance of this marriage succeeding.

In the ceremony I had said, "Marriage is a wonderful gift from God, a way in which two separate lives are brought together and enriched through the experience of a mysterious oneness. But this beautiful relationship will not succeed automatically. It simply will not work well if you do not put your marriage partner's needs before your own."

Did Barbara and Tom hear any of this? They seemed to listen to some of it.

"Success in marriage," I continued, "depends on the capacity of each partner to grow in oneness with the other. Our problem is that it is easy to have oneness as an ideal, but left to ourselves we do not have the power to practice that ideal. It is simply beyond our reach to love another person the way we love ourselves. I know that by myself I do not naturally have the power to love another person with a self-forgetting love that has no price tag on it.

"So often we fail in marriage because we are slow to accept the post-honeymoon reality. The reality is that we bring to marriage two separate wills: I want my way, and my wife wants hers. This is the hidden cause of our conflicts. In each of us there is a self-centered urge to dominate the other, to use the other spouse as a means for selfishly fulfilling our own needs. Since each of us wants his or her way more than anything else in life, we all need a great big intervention of love from outside ourselves to sweeten and renew us. We need God to change our most basic values. Christ is so very willing to do that for us. In his gentleness he comes to us and offers himself as Savior and Lord. He is a living person. From him we can learn to do what is not natural for us—to put the other spouse first. Through trust in him we can find forgiveness for our sins, and out of that forgiveness find our love for the other daily renewed. We can learn to forgive the wrongs done us by the other and to put the other first in our relationships. It's so exciting to see what joy this Jesus can bring into a marriage. But without his presence in a marriage? Well, this kind of unity and love will haunt us as an impossible ideal, and even the ideal will soon get lost in the pressure of human busyness."

My hope was that God would use the realities of the marriage experience to humble this outwardly self-assured couple. But as events soon proved, they resisted him. They acknowledged no need for his "great big intervention of love." Without Christ in their life together, the bonds of married life would soon oppress them. Unfortunately, both Barbara and Tom were captured by the adolescent passion to be happy at all costs. They did not know that there is no surer way to guarantee unhappiness than to pursue happiness for yourself at the expense of others.

You might expect that Barbara with her Christian background would see this. How often the parent of a wandering child looks at the stumblings and says in the heart, "She should know better. She does know better. How can she do these things?" But to expect her to be open to God's wisdom is to expect the blind to have twenty-twenty vision. Barbara could no more understand God's reality than a person born blind could see the sunrise. For she was determined to play the happiness game; all she had eyes for was her own pleasure.

Her constant line now became: "I'm happy at last. Christianity was such a burden. I'm now free from it. So don't expect me to want to return to what made me unhappy." In her proud insecurity she could not afford to admit that she was not being fulfilled by marriage.

Dr. Henry Krabbendam, a good friend of the family and a pastor with a shepherd's heart, visited the young couple in Carlisle some months after their marriage. He wrote to us:

> They were quite cordial but at the same time they wondered out loud whether anyone could add anything to what they had

previously heard from you. Hand-in-hand with the cordiality toward me as a person there was, however, a coldness toward the truth of God as something that seemed totally irrelevant, especially in Barbara. She explained to me that her life had developed from miserable to happy as a result of her decision to turn her back to the truths of God.

In Barbara's mind, "God" and "misery" were synonymous. As far as she was concerned, this was the truth, and for a heart that has not been born again this view of God is reality. There was some truth in it. If God is your unrelenting Judge and you know nothing of the forgiveness of your sins through Jesus' sacrificial death, then your mind will be closed to his love.

Such attitudes can be pretty intimidating to a parent, and it is tempting to say: "You don't look happy." The only result will be to get a big argument going. It is also tempting to withdraw from her and feel sorry for yourself as the abused parent-victim. You can easily end up playing your game while she plays hers.

God, though, does not play games. He was actively pursuing Barbara through our love and through the love of many other Christians. But because he is God, his methods take us by surprise. His delays are especially hard for a father like me to bear. I am a person in a hurry. But vaguely at least I sensed that God's seeming slowness might stem from his having a bigger plan than any of mine. Did he have a much bigger intervention in mind beyond anything I could imagine? Perhaps his purpose was going to take more waiting than I wanted to endure. He was letting our love be treated lightly, taken for granted, and putting our dreams on hold.

During the next year and a half I sensed something of this larger purpose. Certainly, I was disappointed that the outpouring of Christian love at the wedding did not soften Barbara and Tom to Christian things. But it drove *me* back to God. As I prayed and meditated, it dawned on me that what really mattered was not simply seeking Barbara but letting God have the glory in the whole situation. And what would reveal his glory? The answer to that question had now become pretty clear to me. It was by manifesting his love for Barbara no matter what she did. Love that is real love is not pulpy stuff, but it endures—even when it is not received by the other.

Paul says that the law of God commends not just talkers but those "who by persistence in doing good" obey God for the long haul (Romans 2:7). In the Scriptures the quality of endurance or persistence is specifically applied to Jesus, in his life and uniquely to his sufferings in the garden and on the cross. God's Word places great emphasis upon Jesus' refusal to quit when he plunged into the deep waters of his God-appointed suffering. Hebrews 12:2 says, "Let us fix our eyes on Jesus, the author and perfecter of our faith, who for the joy set before him endured the cross, scorning its shame."

The biblical idea is that love is not love unless it knows how to hang on day after day and maybe year after year. Our Lord was not free to say after one hour on the cross, "The price of atoning for sins is too high. I will now come down." No, he persevered in love until he could cry out with triumph, "It is finished." When he made this report of a finished task to his Father, it was because there was nothing left of the Father's will to do.

Similarly as Christians we have a job to do with each of our lives. To get it done, we must endure. As we do, we deepen in our maturity, and see how much we once thought of as love was just sentimental feeling, and that it was exposed as such by our unwillingness to keep on doing it. But God wants our lives to radiate a working love, a love that has the sleeves rolled up and goes on from morning to night. Such love is a good work in God's eyes, and it reveals his glory both to the church and to the world. It also delights his Father's heart. It is nothing less than a sacrifice of praise.

So when Barbara and Tom came to visit, I took time out from our rapidly expanding New Life Church ministry to make friends with Tom. I played chess with him. Rose Marie and I also visited the newlyweds in Carlisle. We attended sports events like lacrosse and baseball when Tom was playing. I talked over books and courses with Barb. She was especially interested in learning Spanish at the time, and I shared her interest. Was this seemingly fruitless persevering wasted? I think not. Love never is. God gave it and God was pleased with it. It was one of the best times of my life, maturing me as a pastor who not only could talk about love but knew something about living it out. There was pain in some of this waiting and enduring. But there was also grace.

Barbara's Response

Since Tom and I were already acting like an old married couple, the logical next step was to make it official, though this was more my doing than Tom's. I saw marriage as the best way to distance myself further from my parents, and to insure an independent existence they could not interfere with. I wanted to be on my own, and with that in mind I decided to quit college and work while Tom continued his schooling. My parents contributed money to my college education, and I wanted even this tie severed.

But I never bothered to consider whether my marriage would succeed. During Thanksgiving vacation, when my father quietly raised some questions about my impending marriage, I blew up. Dad and I were sitting alone at our big oak dining-room table when he brought up the subject. After a few introductory remarks, Dad dropped his bombshell: "I don't see how your marriage to Tom can possibly succeed."

It was like waving a red flag at a bull. I jumped up and shouted, "That's just because we're not Christians. You don't think anything in life works unless someone's a Christian. Well, I'm not going to accept that!" I ran out of the room and started to cry. My father never had a chance to tell me why he thought that our marriage wouldn't work. I went ahead with my plans without another word from my parents on the subject.

The wedding was beautiful. My parents' friends knocked themselves out to make sure the wedding was nice, but I was in a bad mood. My dad witnessed to my two bridesmaids, while I snapped at everyone to get ready and get to the church. Poor Tom bore the brunt of my mood; I was peevish the whole day. The problem was that Tom and I were no longer infatuated, and the reality of what I was doing was beginning to catch up with me. Marriage looked less like a way out and more like another cage. And I would not go to my parents for help.

Back in Carlisle I got a job as a draftsperson. I spent each day drawing tiny lines on large sheets of paper. Every evening I was so exhausted that I would fall into bed after dinner. Tom spent more time with his friends, playing sports and hanging out at the fraternity. I was never good at making friends, and now that we lived off campus, I didn't come into contact with many people at all.

My boredom briefly lifted when we bought a house and spent some time together fixing it up. But when I switched jobs and began working in a typing pool for the State of Pennsylvania, my frustration and feelings of isolation increased. I believed that since I had escaped my parent's religion I could do whatever I wanted. I was supposed to be having a good time, but it grew harder and harder to pretend that I had found happiness. Here I was—living just as I supposed my parents and their friends to be living—having no fun and doing nothing about it. Tom's desire to organize my life was no longer comforting, but oppressive.

My frustration reached a fever pitch on my twenty-first birthday. Tom forgot to buy me a present, I backed my car into a pole, and I came home to an empty house. I wrote a bitter poem about men who ignore their wives' birthdays, and I put my head on the table and cried.

Chapter Five

Free-fall and No Parachute

During September of 1975 Barbara left Tom. She walked into the house looking as gloomy as a week of rainy days and told us. Her account was a bit jumbled. She seemed to be saying, "We're getting a divorce." But she also appeared to be saying that she was the one who wanted it, but Tom was the one getting it.

No matter who initiated the divorce, it meant only one thing: pain. Barbara was hurt. We could see that she still loved Tom, and her love was cutting her like a knife. Her tanned face looked white and strained. I felt the pain of it all with her, and so did Rose Marie. But it was also a relief to see that at least for a moment our daughter was not playing the happiness game. Although I hated to see her suffer, I was encouraged to see the signs of a troubled conscience. She suddenly seemed human and real, and she even conceded that some of the fault was hers. For the first time in over three years she sounded sorry for something.

She went so far as to ask Rose Marie and me for advice— another new development. Torn by conflicting emotions, she asked, "What do you think I should do?"

I asked several questions and finally came to the main point. "Barb, do you want to continue the marriage to Tom?"

She thought for a long and sober moment. We waited. Because I was familiar with Barbara's habit of blame shifting, my question was intended to give the problem back to Barbara for a decision. She desperately needed to take responsibility for her own actions. So we waited and gave no opinion. "Barb," we explained, "you already know what we think about divorce. Do *you* really want this marriage?"

She finally said she still loved Tom.

So I agreed to write him, entreating him to reconsider his decision. In the letter I said Barbara had second thoughts about leaving him and wanted the marriage to continue. I also urged on him, for the first time since their wedding, the importance of taking God's point of view on marriage. I did not expect him to respond. It seemed to me, since Barbara had blamed Rose Marie and I for her problems, that Tom must have been hopelessly prejudiced against us. But it seemed right for me to give reconciliation a try. Maybe something would come of it.

I had a good opinion of Tom. Like Barbara, he was caught up in the moral looseness that characterizes many young people, but he came from a family of morally solid people. In particular, Tom had grown in his disapproval of Barbara's swinging Philadelphia friends, and part of the rupture between Tom and Barbara came because she was beginning to seek them out again.

For our part, experience led us to wonder if Barbara was really telling us the whole story. True, she was stung over Tom's lack of commitment to their vows, but we wondered if there wasn't another side to it. Barbara tended to seek out friends who made up their own marriage rules as they went along. It appeared likely to us that Barbara had been imitating these anarchic role models.

We did not have to wait long for Tom's response. He

proceeded with the divorce, and Barbara took up with her Philadelphia friends. Rose Marie was numb. I was sick at heart. We felt as though Barbara was headed into an abyss and there was nothing we could do to stop it. All we could do was to shake our heads. We had feared the worst and it was beginning to happen. It was like slipping into a bad dream in which you are watching someone about to skydive from an airplane. As the skydiver leans forward to jump, you notice that he is not wearing a parachute. You try to shout a warning, but the cry freezes in your throat. You muster all your strength, but no sound comes. All you can do is watch the skydiver fall.

Again, we were facing the death side of the Christian life, but there was a resurrection ready to take place as we stepped into the grave. Today it is my conviction that no matter how heavy the blow inflicted by circumstances, each negative experience is part of the heavenly Father's perfect plan for each believer. He allows the hour of destruction for the purpose of building something better in its place. Our part is not to run away from the pains but to walk through the briars and thorns and let Christ teach us how to turn each scratch into positive learning about the depths of God's love.

An artist friend of ours illustrated this principle for us one day. He knew how much we admired his superbly landscaped suburban home. Rose Marie and I often praised it as one of the most beautiful settings that we had ever seen. The house sits at the foot of a sloping hill on a piece of level ground that terminates in a quiet stream. The stream runs along the base of a sixty-foot rocky cliff. The hill and the approaches to the house are covered with skillfully arranged paths set among all kinds of trees and shrubs with pines dominating. The house is English medieval in style with a touch of oriental. It is a remarkable union of the wild and the artificial.

As Rose Marie and I expressed our admiration, our friend went inside and brought out some photos. They didn't mean a thing to us at first. They showed some land that had been completely devastated by a bulldozer. You could hardly imagine a more totally ruined setting.

"Do you know where it is?" he asked with a smile.

"Not a clue," we replied.

"You're standing in the middle of it!"

We were dumbfounded. He explained that an artist sometimes has a vision so powerful that it demands a virtual obliteration of the material he is working with. The artist produces chaos to achieve the design he had in view. Something grander, something nobler issues from such artistic destruction than could ever have come from a patchwork piece of landscaping. You need to see the end result to get the full sense of what the artist meant. In essence his point was that the highest art sometimes occurs when the artist imitates his Creator, who formed the glory of creation out of chaos.

That was what God was doing with Barbara, though the idea did not appeal to me then. I hated to watch her fall into a chaos of her own making. Furthermore, I did not like feeling that I was also part of the process of tearing and breaking. I wanted to cry out, "Call off the bulldozer, Lord; I like my landscape just the way it is! I've had my share of suffering."

At that point Rose Marie told me that Jill, our daughter-in-law, and Ruth, our daughter, wanted to talk to me. When I met with Jill, she had some real wisdom to share.

"Ruth and I know how much you and Mom care about Barb," she said. "But we think that the best thing you can do for Barb is to let her go—all the way. Right now she feels the intensity of your caring, but as long as she feels it from you she will not be able to see Christ. You're just too big on the horizon for her to see Jesus."

Later, Ruth said much the same thing. She asked, "Dad, is there anything you need to tell Barbara that you haven't already told her?"

I thought that one over carefully. "No," I answered, "I guess maybe I've said it all at least once and then some." "Then," said Ruth, "ease off. I really believe as you and Mom step back and let her go, you'll give room for the Holy Spirit to work. So long as she feels your emotional pressure, the Holy Spirit can't show her Christ. Now she only feels the presence of you and Mom and all your caring. At this time you have done all you can."

It was a revolutionary idea. It was the kind of wisdom that could only, ultimately, have come from the Lord. I had been taking Barbara so seriously, and unconsciously making her feel my concern, that I was not giving her the opportunity to be driven to Christ by her own mistakes. I was trying to be the Holy Spirit in Barbara's life, and in doing so I only succeeded in making her more aware of me than of God.

The amazing thing was the way our family supported us through this struggle. None of our children ever condemned Barbara or criticized her. Ruth even got me to see the humorous side of the whole thing, and we definitely needed a sense of humor for what unfolded next.

On Christmas Eve Barbara came to our family gathering with a guest. His name was John. Earlier she had prepared the way for this introduction by showing us samples of his photography. It was first-rate, highly original in choice of subjects and photographic precision. It had a stark intensity that was faintly disturbing. Nonetheless, I determined to retain my sense of humor.

Barbara and John arrived in his dark green Jaguar. He wore a black velvet jacket and dark glasses. Good-looking, slim, on the tall side, John carried himself well but looked alert and somewhat wary. When Barbara introduced him, he was gracious with a hint of reserve. And Barbara obviously admired him.

In introducing John, Barbara set forth a tale that lacked plausibility but showed considerable originality. John, she explained, made money by gambling. "He bets," she said, "on professional football games." I had no doubt that he did. The question in my mind was whether he made his living that way. But I kept my mouth shut and rested in the release that I was experiencing as I stood back from Barbara. Whether she knew it or not, she was falling fast and no human being could supply a safety net to catch her.

From that time forward Barbara began to dress expensively and wear rings and bracelets of solid gold. She had found what she wanted—a fitting consort for her role as queen of happiness.

That evening she was determined to prove to us how happy she was. I led the way in extending to John the same warmth and love we had for Barbara. We asked no questions, and he soon ended up laughing and joining in the fun with the rest of us. Soon some of our small grandchildren were sitting in his lap.

While Rose Marie and I still prayed and waited for God's "big intervention," I was satisfied and confident that God was in charge and could be trusted to capture Barbara in his own time and way. For the present I was glad that the dominating schoolmaster that lurks in every father had recently met his death in me when I bowed to the wisdom of Jill and Ruth. The freedom to just treat Barbara as I would any other non-Christian became precious to me. With God's help, I took myself out of the picture. Emotionally, I was freed from destructive conflicts with Barbara and newly opened to learn from God about constructive forms of spiritual conflict. I knew that out of the chaos a new creation would arise, a creation that would glorify Christ.

Barbara's Response

*T*om had become the center of my life. So when life became unbearable, I blamed him. I knew that somewhere there was a world of glamour and excitement—if only I could find it, I believed, I would be happy. I thought I had discovered it when I met John. He was older, more sophisticated, and rich. His possessions revealed his good taste: the expensive sports car, the large home overlooking the countryside, and the pack of exotic hunting dogs. He thought that I'd fit right in, and I certainly wanted to. That his money actually came from drug dealing only added to his allure.

So I left Tom and began a new life with John. The external aspects of my life were now very different. I no longer had to get up at six in the morning to type memos about waste-disposal sites, and I no longer had to worry about the bills at the end of the month. Instead, we spent our time going out to gourmet restaurants, buying expensive presents for ourselves and others, and flying at a moment's notice to Florida where John would conduct business. My family had always joked that I was the type of person who should have peaches and cream served to her every morning. Although I laughed, I secretly believed it. I deserved that kind of life and now I had it. Imagine my happiness when John hired a houseman. Now I didn't have to do anything I didn't want to.

At first the only cloud on the horizon was the reaction of

71

my family and friends. Everyone was horrified. I had left Tom and moved in with a drug dealer who carried money in his briefcase and a gun in his belt. My friend Sally came down for the weekend with her boyfriend, who was so shocked by the stacks of money, the guns, and the rented cars in the driveway that he hitchhiked home in the middle of the night. Another friend, Betsy, came to visit and never contacted me again. Years later she confided that John scared her to death; around him she always felt that her life was in danger.

My family was low key but obviously uneasy. In the course of our first evening together, we offered three explanations for how John earned his money. We said that (a) he was a house painter, (b) he was a photographer, and (c) he was a professional gambler. Unfortunately, my brother, who painted houses for a living, was curious to know why he was making so much less than John. He questioned John about his methods while his wife, Jill, kicked him under the table. One of my brothers-in-law, Jim, is an amateur photographer, and although he sat quietly while John showed his work, I could see that he knew these pictures were not a professional's portfolio. They were good, but not that good. As a last resort we told them that John was a professional gambler. Since no more questions were asked, I assumed that my family either believed us or were no longer interested in digging out the truth.

But another, blacker cloud was my broken relationship with Tom. Although I portrayed Tom in the worst possible light to my family, in my heart I knew that I was responsible for the breakup of our marriage. He had been faithful; I had not. Even later, when I learned that Tom was living with another woman, I was heartbroken. As I continued living with John, I wanted Tom back and would have long phone conversations with him in which I tried to convince him to give our marriage another try. I didn't need my friends to point out how irrational this was; I could see it for myself. In desperation I went to a psychologist.

My therapist listened quietly while I told her about my confusion and how my parents' religious beliefs were still ruining my life. The quieter she became the more verbose I got. I wondered when I was going to start getting the sympathy I deserved for the way my parents had made me feel guilty for everything I did. Her only response was that she wasn't interested in my past but in how I was handling my present. What a disappointment! My weekly sessions became harder for me as I worked for the sympathy that I never got.

So when John suggested moving to the Pocono Mountains I eagerly agreed.

Chapter Six

Forgiveness as a Lifestyle

One day Lisa, a friend of Barbara's, called. She thought it was a shame to see Barbara and me estranged from each other; Barbara, she said, was ready for reconciliation if I was. I thanked her and turned the idea over in my mind.

Although she did not say it directly, the implication was that Barbara was angry with me. It would have been natural for me to have said, "Look, I'm the wounded party here. If there's to be any reconciliation, it should begin with Barbara." Yet I knew that the Bible clearly teaches that if we know we've offended someone it is our duty to seek that person out and attempt to remove the cause of offense (Matthew 5:21–26).

It is foolish to think that you can live with a child for eighteen years without committing plenty of sins against that child. Think only of the obvious things—the occasional lack of affection, the coldness of manner, being too busy to listen to problems and hurts—and you realize that a young person who has not learned to forgive must carry a pretty heavy bag of grudges.

So I swallowed my fears, claimed the promise of the Spirit's presence by faith, and asked Barbara for a talk. We walked to a small bridge in Melrose Park. After chatting a bit, I said,

"Barb, I think you have some things against me, maybe things I need to correct."

After only a slight hesitation, she replied, "I do. When I was growing up, you were always my hero. In my eyes you were perfect." She paused.

My memory flashed back to the early years of Barbara's life. In Ripon, California, where I taught high-school English, we would often go for family drives after school. In our '52 Buick, as we drove toward the Sierra Nevada foothills or to the Stanislau River for a swim, Barbara would stand on the seat next to me, her arm on my shoulder. Barb was my friend. Like the rest of our children she absorbed all I could tell about fairy tales, *The Iliad* and *The Odyssey*, Bible stories, and the Shorter Catechism. Rose Marie led us in hymns. I knew I had been Barbara's idol.

"When I grew older," she continued, "it came to me that no one could be that perfect. So as a teenager when I saw your weaknesses, I didn't know how to handle it. When any problem came up, any crisis, you were always the one who knew what to do. As long as I can remember, there was a circle of admirers around you. And I knew no one is that perfect, that together all the time."

I could feel the anger behind her words.

"Barb," I said, "I'm really sorry for that. I'm *not* perfect, and I regret giving the impression that I thought I was. I know there were many times that in my heart I didn't have answers, and I should have told you so. Will you forgive me?"

The anger melted from her face, and she threw her arms around me and sobbed. "I do forgive you, I do!"

It was a beautiful moment—God's gift, made possible by his love working in our lives in answer to many prayers. It was an example of constructive conflict at its best. My natural way of doing things would have been to try to straighten out her moral life, to get her to stay away from people like John, and to give up the gold jewelry and the expensive clothing.

76

But at this stage, without first being reconciled I would have done nothing but deepen our estrangement. What she needed from me was the knowledge that I loved her unconditionally. That is the most powerful weapon in the parent's arsenal, and the only weapon that can really touch the hardened conscience of a deeply rebellious spirit.

It was to this subject that Barbara immediately turned. "Dad, I want to know that you love me—unconditionally!"

"I do," I said, "and will try to keep doing it."

The conversation moved on, and eager to see her experience further liberation, I asked her, "Are there other people that you are angry with?"

After several minutes, Barbara named several people in the Christian community who had angered her. She was especially bitter against two Christian school teachers.

This disclosure immediately precipitated a crisis. You could see from the way she talked that she was still upset by some things these teachers had done. I suggested that she should forgive them along with the others she had mentioned. But her problem was that she had rejected God and his truth, and forgiveness only makes sense within that framework. It was a painful crisis for her. How do you forgive someone when you reject the whole idea of being sinned against—the idea that there is a law of God that has been broken?

"I don't see how I can forgive them," she answered. "But I agree I need to. My bitterness against them—I need to get rid of it."

I was not unsympathetic. Hers was a real dilemma, one that faces all people who reject the rule of God over their lives. How do you live in a world that really does not make much sense unless you presuppose God's sovereignty over it? Of course, I don't think Barbara was actually an atheist or an agnostic. She had simply worked to kill the awareness of God in herself, and up to that point she had been doing a good job of it. But to forgive, she had to move onto borrowed ground—she had to move into Christ's kingdom. Not only would she have to act as though God existed, she would also have to act as though his rules for living—like the one requiring us to forgive others—applied to her. In other words, to forgive the teachers would represent something like a submission to God.

"Perhaps," I said, "you shouldn't try to figure it all out. Just go ahead and forgive them."

"I don't know how, or maybe I don't want to. Look, Dad, it doesn't make sense, but I'll try."

Then I led her like a little child through the list of names. As I mentioned each name, I said, "I forgive you," and I had Barbara repeat everything after me. Soon she looked relieved. I could see that much of the bitterness had drained out of her. It confirmed my conviction that God's principles for ordering human life work when nothing else will.

Our relationship seemed to enter a new stage. We were friends again, but without the old illusions. We were building a friendship based upon truth, and it was a lovely thing.

This new bond also gave me a new freedom in speaking to Barbara from the heart. Under what I believe was God's compulsion, I said to Barbara before we parted, "Barb, there's something I want you to know, though we don't need to discuss it. It's that I forgive you too. I forgive you for anything that you have done against me."

It was said gently and with love. She looked very thoughtful. Startled perhaps? I did not know. Little did I know that this act would initiate a whole new train of thought in Barbara's mind, leading to very positive changes.

Although I know some Christians will have problems with what was done at the little bridge in Melrose Park, I saw it as the first signs of spring in the winter of Barbara's life. To some believers it may seem unbiblical. They might say, "You cannot forgive someone who has sinned against you until they have repented." Some even go so far as to say that you should not forgive until the person has demonstrated repentance over a period of time by way of a changed life. What they fail to see is that forgiveness too has stages. At first you forgive the person who has not changed and persists in evil behavior. You forgive in the hope that in time the person will repent. Next you deepen your forgiveness when the person expresses repentance and shows the fruit of a changed life. At this stage you welcome the repentant person fully into your fellowship.

According to the Scriptures, forgiveness goes to the very heart of the new covenant that Jesus established in his atoning death for our sins. Through faith in Jesus' death, the believer's sins have been forgiven. It is God's free gift, and the believer takes it up as a distinctive lifestyle, covering the whole range of emotions and relationships. Forgiven by God, the believer can then forgive others (Matthew 26:28). In fact, the believer is expected to forgive at all times and from the heart (Matthew 18:21–35; 6:12, 14; Mark 11:25). On the cross, Jesus forgave his enemies while they were still gloating and even though we have no evidence that they ever repented for their wrongs (Luke 23:34). Similarly, when Stephen interceded for his persecutors at the time of his martyrdom, there was not the slightest hint of remorse among them (Acts 7:60). In spite of their wickedness he exhibited not only a loving spirit, but he also entreated God to forgive them.

There is another, often hidden issue in the picture. It is this: The practice of comprehensive forgiveness overcomes our own love of being right, our actual enjoyment and treasuring of our sense of being wronged. I knew I had to root these feelings out of my life if I was going to succeed in my conflict with Barbara. And we were in conflict. Don't think we were not! We were soldiers serving different leaders, and I desperately needed to use only the weapons appointed by my Commander. The constant practice of forgiveness leaves no room for self-righteousness. Frustrated condemnation of others and treasuring of old wrongs are not part of the artillery of God, but the slithering, slimy, deadly creatures of the Prince of Darkness.

The problem with an unforgiving bitterness is that it is a concealed root that can go deep into the life without the person possessed by it knowing that it is there. When this happens, prayer becomes ineffectual because the Spirit is grieved by our lack of forgiveness (Ephesians 4:30–5:2).

Look at it from God's point of view. When you ask him to intervene and save an erring child, you are, in effect, saying, "God, work in my son's life so that he may be received into your heaven. Don't condemn my son. Forgive him and save him." But God sees your heart. What does he see in it? The very opposite of what you prayed for. You ask him to forgive a son or daughter, but your spirit is filled with memories of many wrongs done to you. You feel sorry for yourself for all that your wayward child has made you suffer. You have not, in fact, forgiven your own John or Barbara. You say, "I will forgive when I see repentance first, but not until." How do you suppose God is able to answer prayers that are offered with that spirit?

A few years ago I was asked by a Christian mother to pray for her daughter Terissa. The sad story of Terissa's rebelliousness was detailed for me. But as the tale unfolded, I wondered if that was the whole story.

I asked with as much love as I could muster, "Suppose Terissa returned today and said she was sorry. Would she be welcomed by the family?"

A strange look came across the woman's face. "Of course not," she said. "There's too much hurt in the family, too much bitterness against her. We just couldn't welcome her."

Wanting to exercise charity, I asked if the family would simply need more time to adjust to the repentant Terissa. To my surprise, the woman shook her head. She was not sure that the family would ever be able to forgive and forget. At least she was honest. It was clear that what really bothered this family was its having been betrayed by a once-loyal member. The vision of that betrayal crowded out the love of God. The members of that family seemed to have fallen in love with their own wounds.

I told the woman that I believed her family needed to repent perhaps even more than Terissa. I assured her of my love and right there invited her to join me in praying for her wayward family as well as for her wayward daughter. My hope was that God in his grace would bring the *whole* family to a new vision of the forgiving grace of God.

In God's providence, when parents are faced with the bitter experience of a child's long-term betrayal, it represents an opportunity to learn new and wonderful things about God's approach to forgiveness. To learn his approach, study the Scripture passages on forgiveness listed in this chapter. Then engage in some healthy self-examination. You don't want things cooking in the basement of your life that are sending poisonous fumes silently and insidiously into the living quarters of your life.

Ask the Father to give you the Holy Spirit to search you out and to reveal what is cooking in the basement of your life. After all, if the basement is clean, you have nothing to fear. But if not, you need to start mopping up all the bitter messes in your life and let in the fresh air of forgiveness.

Barbara's Response

*B*efore leaving for the Poconos with John, I visited some friends in Philadelphia, in an old stone house in Melrose Park. As I relaxed in one of the upstairs bedrooms, my friend Lisa came up and said, "Your father's here to see you."

I had mixed feelings as I walked down the steps to greet him, though I was touched that he would seek me out, especially here, where everything that went on was diametrically opposed to his own beliefs and actions. But I wondered what he wanted. I felt like I did when I was a young child and I would hear him call, "Barbara Catherine, come here right now!" from the bottom of the stairs. The use of my middle name was always a tip-off that I was in big trouble. Was he silently calling "Barbara Catherine" now? I didn't know, so I steeled myself for the worst.

After we greeted each other, he asked me to go for a walk. We chatted about everyday occurrences until we reached a little bridge. We stopped, and as I nervously threw twigs into the water, my father shocked me by asking, "Do you have anything that you need to forgive me for?" I had a lot, but for a moment I was stunned. I had rarely seen my father admit that he had ever done anything wrong. In our family, he mainly worked with us until we confessed *our* sins. That was what I had against him. I knew his sins—after all, I lived with him for eighteen years—but I had no sense that he could ever admit any of his weaknesses to his family. My mother handled conflict with Dad by having allergy attacks. In my naïve eyes, my father deserved the blame for my mother's weakness. When I explained some of this to him, I was further shocked when he asked me to forgive him. I think that we both cried as I said that I forgave him, and we hugged.

Conversations with my dad often have a certain good-news−bad-news quality, and this conversation was no different. After I forgave him, he said that he had something to forgive me for. He told me that he forgave me for the way I had turned my back on him and my mother when they dropped me off at Dickinson College. It was news to me that I had hurt them. At first I was miffed that he would have the nerve to forgive me for something that I didn't even know I had done. But as I thought about it, my conscience began to bother me. *Was it possible,* I wondered, *that my parents were human too? Did they have feelings that could be hurt just like mine?* These were new ideas to me.

Soon after this conversation, I moved to the Poconos. Even though I was now physically further away from my family, I felt closer to them emotionally. For the first time I felt my parents accepted me for who I was, instead of for who they wanted me to be. My father, by confessing that he had made mistakes, became more human to me. I was starting to feel comfortable again in my own family.

At Grandfather's ranch in Bolinas, California, 1953. The first four Miller children, *l. to r.*: Barbara, 2; Paul, 3; Ruth, 4; Roseann 5.

The Miller family in front of our home in Jenkintown, Pennsylvania in 1968—the house where we still live. *Seated l. to r.*: Barbara, 14; Ruth, 16. *Standing l. to r.*: Keren, 8; Roseann, 17; Paul, 15; Rosemarie; and Jack.

January 1974. Barbara greeting friends after her marriage to Tom.

Angelo Juliani in 1973. When Barbara moved in with Angelo, the first thing she did was to throw out this pink jacket.

Barbara and Rose Marie watching a basketball game in 1976.

Christmas 1975. The Miller family plus in-laws and grandchildren. *Seated l. to r.*: Aunt Barbara, Grandma Carlsen (Ashley Miller in lap), Jack Miller, Rose Marie Miller (Kimiko Trott on lap), Keren Miller (Courtney on lap), Barbara Miller. *Standing l. to r.*: Jim Correnti, Ruth Correnti, Roseann Trott, Jim Trott, Paul Miller, Jill Miller.

Jack Miller while street preaching in Ireland in 1984.

Gabriel Juliani's christening in 1986, with Mary Juliani (Angelo's mom), Barbara, and Angelo Juliani, Sr.

Jack and Rose Marie Miller at a banquet in their honor in 1986.

Halloween 1987. Barbara, Angelo, Gabriel, and AJ Juliani going trick-or-treating at a friend's house.

Angelo, Barbara, and youngest son, Gabriel, on Christmas Day 1986.

Chapter Seven

Praying as Sons of the Father

*T*he big chrome and glass tour bus picked us up at the Geneva airport. In a few short hours it brought nearly thirty of us Americans through Lausanne and over the mountains to Gstaad. As we eased around the last of the mountain turns, we could see the village of Château d'Oèx below us. It was spread out in a broad valley surrounded by forested mountains. As we drew nearer we could see chalets decorating the hillsides. At its center, the small town was dominated by a hill on which stood a stone church and its supporting buildings. Near the church, the bus parked in front of a hotel styled along the lines of a large chalet. This was our destination.

I had some doubts about this trip. At the time I had a big plateful of responsibilities at home: teaching full time at Westminster Theological Seminary, pastoring the rapidly growing New Life Church, and doing evangelistic work with the Presbyterian Evangelistic Fellowship. And of course, my concern for Barbara was constant. What was I doing speaking at a conference in Switzerland? Little did I know that God would use this conference to mobilize new spiritual resources in the fight to claim Barbara for Christ—and Rose Marie and I needed more help than any human being could supply.

It had been my hope that the reconciliation between Barbara and me would result in immediate changes in her life. My hope was soon shattered on the hard rocks of reality when Barbara began to travel widely with John and people like him. First she was in Florida, next in Puerto Rico, and then in the Bahamas. By early March of 1976, John had given her a lovely fur coat. It went well with the heavy gold rings and bracelets.

The whole business made Rose Marie and me uneasy at best. We tried to bear with Barbara and her friends, but we were not always sure where to draw the line. It was humbling to feel so far out of our depth. Many parents see this as a great disadvantage and resent being put into a situation where it is clear that they are not in control. I think this is a mistake rooted in our desire to appear wise and knowing before our children.

Therefore, even though we did not know what to do, we decided that if we had to err we should do so on the side of openness and friendship. We even went to the Poconos to ski with Barbara and John. Always loyal, Paul and Jill came along, and it proved to be a good time for all. Of course, the signs of wealth that surrounded John did not ease our concerns. He had a beautiful house, four expensive vehicles, and several expensive hunting dogs—Rhodesian ridge-backs—that were big, powerful, and unusually fast. One of them even made friends with me.

Barbara told us she was happy, which actually made me sick at heart for we knew that she was in over her head and seemingly unaware of the growing power of evil in her life. When I thought about her and John, I could have cried.

Our family had always observed strict rules against gossip, but it was impossible not to continue our speculations over John's occupation. Did he gamble? Probably. But I come from gambling country, and I never met anyone who actually became rich through gambling except, of course, casino owners. John did not claim an interest in anything of that kind. Was he involved in prostitution? He did not seem the type somehow, but maybe. Smuggling? Drugs? The last seemed most likely.

The more we thought about John, the mystery man, the more we felt that Barbara was in danger. For us to insist that she leave John, however, would most likely cause her to react by plunging even more deeply into this high-flying lifestyle.

So we tried to soothe our nerves, keep our mouths shut, and wait. Waiting in a godly way, without frustration but in prayerful dependence on God, is not easy, believe me. Waiting for God to intervene is a kind of death, a special humiliation to activistic Americans like us. We always want to be *doing* something, finding some new how-to as a means for providing instant release from our struggles. But I was slowly getting the idea that God wanted us to meet him, and let him meet Barbara in his own way and in his own time.

We knew that John had not entrapped Barbara and that the real chain by which the devil held her was her own mental outlook. Like many young people, she was convinced, with an almost religious intensity, that the most important thing in life is seeking fulfillment and that the worst thing is to be unhappy—and the worst form of unhappiness is boredom. Barbara hated boredom. She had left Tom because marriage had become dull and routine. She had taken up with John because his life looked exciting and her adolescent imagination could not conceive of anything bad happening through her involvement with him. The idea that life with John might have some danger in it just added piquancy to the dish of her happiness.

At this critical point Rose Marie suddenly became an active campaigner in the long struggle for Barbara's life. It began at the conference in Switzerland. I have said comparatively little about Rose Marie's role in the seeking of Barbara up to this point. There was a good reason for this. Until God met with her in Switzerland, Rose Marie was still pretty much in what she called the state of being "numb." Hard hit by Barbara's departure, Rose Marie had her own struggles, compounded by bodily weaknesses that began with major surgery early in 1972. So for the first three years she left the pursuit of Barbara largely to me.

To understand the change in her life, you need some idea of what went on at the conference. It was organized by Harold Morris, a leader in the Presbyterian Evangelistic Fellowship, and it focused on the theme of "Sonship and Freedom in Christ." I gave a series of lectures on this topic, drawing material from Exodus and Galatians. James Smith, a family counselor then working with PEF, drew out the implications of this material for family living. He was especially effective in explaining how "putting on" a lifestyle of forgiveness and blessing could transform family relationships.

But Harold, our hard-working conference director, came down with the flu and was confined to bed, which meant that I was suddenly made acting director for the conference. When several other participants came down with the flu, I tried to play doctor as well. Every morning and evening I held forth on the Christian's sonship in the beautiful conference room. To my right the majestic Alps could be seen through a long, high window that ran almost the whole length of the room. This natural testimony to the greatness of God strengthened my faith, and encouraged me to continue with my series of messages on the power of faith to bring the adopted sons of God release from guilt and fullness of joy through fellowship with the Father.

Rose Marie, who has an honest heart, said, "Your messages don't mean a thing to me. I don't feel forgiven, and I don't feel like 'a son of God.' Tell me what to do. Give me some how-tos." James Smith and I gave her a few "how-tos," but they didn't seem to help much. So we gave up in frustration.

But on Thursday of that week she had a breakthrough, one of those happy deaths that I had been having, the kind that kills something so deep inside you that it leads to an unexpected resurrection.

Rose Marie had gone skiing, while I spent the afternoon walking, meditating, and praying in the village. Having just come from the church on the hill, I wondered where she was. A little before six that evening I saw her, a solitary figure, trudging down the snow-covered road. I quickly set off to meet her.

"How was the skiing?" I called. She moved stiffly, almost as though she had no knees.

She responded with a funny look and said, "Awful, just awful. I can't believe it!"

"Where did you go?"

"Up there," she said, and pointed in the general direction of the Alps. I looked. "No," she said, "not up there. Over there."

My mouth fell open. "You mean you went up on that mountain to ski?" It looked to me as though she had been on the top of the world. "Dear me," I groaned, "I wouldn't even ride the gondola that high, much less ski up there."

At the hotel I ran a hot bath for her and helped her into it. Her story tumbled out between groans. She had taken the gondola to the highest level and from there had gone even higher on another lift. From the top she looked down on the steep slopes and saw that the snow was frozen glass. Instead of returning, however, she set off down the slope only to fall and lose a ski. Then she took off the other ski to climb down the mountain in pursuit of the runaway ski. Her feet kept breaking through the icy crust. She would fall and struggle to her feet, only to fall again. After a long time she finally managed to board the gondola. She was a "battered wreck."

That Sunday I spoke again about the joys of sonship. During Communion, a large loaf of French bread was broken. It had a solid crust and made a "crack" that could be clearly

89

heard as it broke. Somehow, through that noise, that crack, God spoke to Rose Marie.

As she put it later, "Before that I had never seen myself as a real sinner. I'm descended from several generations of Lutheran ministers, and all that religious goodness left me with no sense of sin. But when that bread cracked, I suddenly saw that Christ's body was broken for my sins and that my biggest sin was my self-righteousness. My chaotic descent down the ski slope was a picture of my life, a life filled with self-righteous presumption rather than faith. I was so proud that I even blamed God for letting me fall on the slope. I now began to see that it was my fault. I could have prevented the whole thing simply by going back down the way I came up. I now knew that my sin was my independent attitude, my self-righteousness.

"When Jack preached on 'Amazing Grace' that Sunday morning, I saw Christ broken for me. For the first time in my life I had a conviction of sin. I saw my sin as against God now. I saw real evil in my self-will. But before that Communion service I saw myself as basically a good person with a few flaws. I had felt guilt before—lots of it and all the time—but it was guilt over my failures more than guilt because I had sinned against God. I was utterly humbled now that my sins were all forgiven because Christ had died for me. He loved me—me, the unloving one. I longed to know more about him from the depths of my heart."

When we returned to Philadelphia, Rose Marie's life began to manifest a freedom and joy that had never been there before. About two years earlier, to help her understand what justification by faith and sonship were all about, I had photocopied Martin Luther's introduction to his Galatians commentary. Intellectually she knew all about the Reformation teaching that free pardon and acceptance are granted to the sinner through the crediting of Christ's righteousness to the sinner's account by faith alone. But it had never touched her inner life. "Before Switzerland," she said, "I couldn't understand what Luther meant by 'passive righteousness' because I was so filled with my own 'active righteousness.' I was a self-righteous orphan, not a son of the Father. But once I deliberately trusted in the righteousness of Christ, you can't imagine how different my view of God became. It especially changed my whole approach to prayer. Now I had sure confidence that my Father really heard my cries. *Confidence* is the word—praying with the simplicity of a child and yet with the authority of a son."

Friends have asked Rose Marie, "Were you converted in Switzerland? Weren't you a Christian before then?"

She usually answers, "I don't know and I don't worry about it. I'm just glad I didn't die in my previous state, with all my legalism. My guess is that I was a Christian but was so ignorant about God's grace that I functioned in my inner life almost entirely as a non-Christian would. Who knows?"

The immediate fruit of Rose Marie's renewal was that both of us experienced a new authority in prayer. Throughout 1976 Barbara had teetered on the edge of a cliff but was kept from falling by prayer alone. Instead of giving up, I kept recruiting people to pray for her. Because I was associated with Presbyterian Evangelistic Fellowship as an evangelist, I was greatly encouraged in my faith to know that many brothers and sisters were interceding for her. I also became better acquainted with Donald B. McNair, a missions leader of the then Reformed Presbyterian Church, Evangelical Synod, through his teaching in my classes at Westminster Theological Seminary. He and I pledged ourselves to pray each for the other's children. Knowing he was praying meant a great deal to me.

In Philadelphia, Rose Marie now led the way with boldness in praying for Barbara. She claimed in prayer a passage from Hosea, which reads: "Behold, I will hedge up thy way with thorns, and make a wall, that she shall not find her paths. And she shall follow after her lovers, but she shall not overtake them; and she shall seek them, but shall not find them: then she shall say, I will go and return to my first husband; for then was it better with me than now" (Hosea 2:6–7 KJV).

When Barbara became repeatedly ill during the rest of 1976, she eventually came to us and asked for prayers for healing. I cannot overstate how big a change this was for Barbara—to humble herself in this way before us, her parents. Things also began to go sour in her relationship with John. He became almost insanely jealous, and by the end of the year Barbara was ready to admit that their relationship was a disaster.

Prayer is everything in the Christian life. When it is offered with confident authority by those who are self-consciously relying as sons on their Father, big developments follow. So now our prayers were being heard in a remarkable way by a loving heavenly Parent. Because God was responding to our prayers, Barbara was also learning about life and God. She was beginning to feel what Francis Thompson confesses in his poem "The Hound of Heaven" when Christ says, "All things betray thee who betrayest Me."

Barbara's Response

As I grew more comfortable with my family, I grew increasingly less comfortable with John. Things were not working out. The world of drug dealing that had looked so exciting before was proving to be quite dull. Because of the need for secrecy about John's "business" we had few friends, and the friends we did have were mostly dealers who were too paranoid to even have a normal conversation with me. As a minister's daughter, I knew how to draw people out with questions. But John's friends thought I was prying and wondered if I was a narcotics agent. So much for making friends!

As I got to know them better, I realized that they were not people I would have picked for friends anyway. As a result of their paranoia, they surrounded themselves with dogs, guns, and faithful retainers. Their conversations, influenced by drugs and alcohol, were uninspired at best and mainly revolved around themselves and the price of marijuana. I was not impressed. Many nights I would sit reading spy novels or gothic romances while everybody else got high and made desultory conversation.

My relationship with John was also not as fun as when we first met. He was charming and worldly, but underneath it all he was insecure. For instance, he began to feel that perhaps I was more committed to the things that he could give me than

I was to him personally. This led to long intense fights that, fueled by cocaine, would last all night. His fear that I would leave him led him to be paranoid every time I left the house. On a couple of occasions he even followed me to make sure that I wasn't meeting another man. I coped with this by staying at home simply to avoid conflict. He would go away for days at a time and I would do nothing but take care of the dogs. It snowed a lot that winter, and many days I would not even venture outside unless I had to go look for the dogs. For many hours the ridgebacks were my only company and the phone was my only lifeline to the outside world. My dream life had become a nightmare.

I thought about leaving, but my own insecurities chained me to John. My surface worries were material. I could not face the thought of working again as a secretary and having to scrape for every dollar. But underlying this were my same old fears and insecurities. Only now, these problems were magnified by the time that I had spent with John. Our isolated and paranoid lifestyle had encouraged me to think less and less of my own abilities. I believed that I could no longer cope on my own. I was so afraid of meeting new people or of being in any new situation that I was even afraid of going to new restaurants. I was afraid of everything and everybody, and was close to a nervous breakdown. I wanted to leave John but was paralyzed by fear.

The one bright spot in my life was my family. Although John never felt completely at ease around them, I did. They came to visit and their phone calls provided me with much needed companionship. I began to share my problems with them, and they listened without offering much advice. In contrast to mine, their lives seemed sane—and happy.

Chapter Eight

Learning to Pray with Authority

*B*efore Switzerland, Rose Marie and I had prayed along these lines: "Lord, save Barbara" or "Father, make her a Christian" or "God, protect her from evil and bring her back to us." Although any prayer is probably better than none, battle-weary parents can forget that effective prayer requires the best thought we can bring to it. Without issues being searched out by wisdom based upon the Scriptures, we are likely to pray timid, vague half-prayers. Although these lame prayers are offered repeatedly, nothing seems to happen, perhaps because nothing is expected to happen.

But after God's encounter with Rose Marie in Switzerland, our faith was buoyed by her taste of the riches of God's fatherhood. Rose Marie especially began to pray for Barbara with new confidence and with a new authority arising from her position *in* Christ and her possession *of* the Spirit of the Father. Out of her meditation of Romans and Galatians there came to her prayers a strong note of sonship boldness, a humble but almost prophetic challenge for God to fulfill his word. She was reasoning with God as a child of the Father, urging him to keep his covenant promise to save the families of believers (Genesis 17:7; Psalm 78:1–8; Acts 2:38–39; 16:31).

In all of this there was also a surprise. This new authority in praying for Barbara also began to expose a weakness in our whole approach to our intercession for her. As we based our prayers more on the promises of the Father, we discovered something in our mental image of Barbara that had been so much a part of our thinking that we had hardly noticed it.

What goes on in the minds of battered parents when it comes time to pray? Often a sense of defeat takes over the spirit, a cloud that can descend even when the parents have forgiven the young person and have real love in their hearts. The problem is that parents often have a fixed negative image of the child. He or she is seen as unchangeable, an image that may be powerfully reinforced by the recollection of the adolescent's many failings: repeated acts of rebellion, words of rebellion, and looks of rebellion.

The devil knows how to use this image to undermine effective prayer. He suggests to the unsuspecting parent that this image of cold resistance is the *final* vision of the child. "This thankless child cannot be changed," says the Master of Darkness. Listening uncritically to this voice, the praying father or mother then naturally lets the mind become fixed on the child's stubbornness. Who can pray effectively when the mind is clouded by this picture of steely resistance?

To overcome this, simply shift the mind to the promises of divine grace found in the Scriptures. As a parent, focus your faith by meditating on a great biblical passage like Luke 15, in which you see the great images of faith. You discover the Father's grace in action. Lost things do not remain lost; they are found. The dead come alive. The lost sheep is found by the shepherd, the lost coin by the housewife, and the lost son is welcomed home with almost scandalous warmth by a loving father. When you think about these things, you will realize that the Father loves even you, the parent, as a lost child that has been found. Will he not love your child the same way?

In Luke 15:11–32 you find a window opening into heaven itself in the parable of the lost son. You see a formerly rebellious son heading home, drawn by a father's irresistible love. As I strain to see through this window, I see a father carried away with love, impelled by compassion for the lost, and going out the gate as fast as his legs can run. Of course, it is an earthly setting, but it is also a revelation of the power and love of God reaching out and transforming the most unwilling of human beings into children of the Father.

The Christian parent must read this parable and believe that it describes the future of the erring son or daughter. He or she must see that the God of the Bible has the heart and the skills to turn a dead, lost, crazy rebel into a living, sane human being. This is the image that God wants to dominate our minds as we pray. We need to know that his great heart is filled with active love, drawing to himself the Augustines, the John Bunyans, and John Newtons, and the Barbaras. How beautiful they become! How bright they shine with his love when he brings them to himself!

Remember too that he also has the power to make them into the new image of the living son of God. When this vision fills the mind, who cannot pray effectively for the most stubborn rebel?

Having learned to pray with more authority, we also began to pray more specifically for Barbara. With emphatic agreement Rose Marie and I asked God to expose Barbara to the thorns of life and use their sharp points to drive her out of her evil nest in the Poconos. We finally gathered our courage and asked God to make life so unbearable with John that she would want to leave him. God heard that prayer early in 1977, as I noted earlier. For months Barbara had had so much restlessness, so much sickness, so much tussle with living with John that she finally decided to give it all up.

97

"All of a sudden I left," she said later. "The whole way of life was awful. He was mixing all kinds of drugs, and the lifestyle and cocaine made him paranoid. He was really trying to take me further away from my family. I must have been crazy to have taken it so long."

What was equally important was that Barbara was actually getting an overdose of her glitter mania. At last she knew that happiness did not consist of spending a couple of thousand dollars on clothes and driving off in a green Jaguar. We Americans sometimes have trouble getting over our adolescence; Barbara's was being squeezed out of her right down to the last drop. The pain must have been terrible, but the results were liberating.

Encouraged by these developments, we prayed with even more effectiveness for our daughter. About this time we encountered a tract issued by the Back to the Bible Broadcast entitled "How I Learned to Pray for the Lost." It is a short discussion of the importance of learning to pray with authority for lost members of your family. It especially focused on the importance of praying for the mental life of the unconverted person. It emphasizes that demonic influence blinds the hearts of non-Christians. A key passage in the tract states:

> To pray in the name of the Lord Jesus is to ask for, or to claim, the things which the blood of Christ has secured. Therefore, each individual for whom prayer is made should be claimed by name as God's purchased possession, in the name of the Lord Jesus Christ and on the basis of His shed blood.
>
> We should claim the tearing down of all the works of Satan, such as false doctrine, unbelief, atheistic teaching and hatred, which the Enemy may have built up in their thinking. We must pray that their very thoughts will be brought into captivity to Christ.

Rose Marie and I found this brief essay stimulating to our faith. Yet we were not quite sure what to do about it. We first read the pamphlet at a conference in Houston, Texas. Between sessions, Rose Marie and I went for a walk down one of the city streets. We asked ourselves, "What exactly are Barb's crucial areas of blindness? What are the major bonds that are holding her prisoner?"

We came up with four areas of sin in her young life: (1) deceiving and lying, (2) dishonesty as a way of life, (3) sensualism, and (4) excuse-making. Barbara was bound in such a deep way by these things that she hardly seemed aware they were there.

While walking down that Houston street, I led us in four simple prayers, offered quietly and without much emotion. The first was: "Holy Father, in the authority of Jesus' name we ask you to rebuke any demonic power or powers blinding Barbara, holding her captive in deception and lying. We ask you to open her mind to see that deceiving and lying are wrong. We entreat you to bring her to repentance for these sins and to be cleansed by trusting in Christ's gospel. We now thank you for hearing this prayer. Amen."

We were asking God to arouse Barbara's conscience so that she would begin to see specific evils for what they were, to hate them, and to turn to Christ for cleansing from their guilt and power.

We did the same for the other three areas of blindness. The whole prayer could not have lasted more than ten or fifteen minutes. We told no one about it, especially not Barbara. We did not rush home and ask Barbara if she was changed. In fact, once having prayed in this specific and authoritative way, we forgot about it.

I do not offer this kind of prayer as a religious gimmick, a spiritual rabbit's foot, or a mechanical formula for pious insiders. To think we are offering something like that would be a ghastly mistake. The important thing is that our prayer occurred within the framework of an aggressive love carried out not in our own strength or wisdom but by relying on the promises of God. This kind of authoritative prayer was the climax of a lengthy program of God's humbling us, releasing us from many of our own bonds and fears, and revealing to us the wonder of the Reformation doctrine of free justification by faith and the rights of the sons of God.

In the spring of 1977, after leaving John, Barbara came home. During that time she deepened her friendship with the rest of us and returned to college. As she told me about her courses at Temple, her professors' ideas, and her papers, I was able to share my own insights. Though political science is not my field, I had read widely and was able to talk with her and to be a friend.

One day in late spring or early summer Rose Marie found Barbara sitting at the picnic table on our back porch. She sat down beside Barbara and, since the moment seemed natural, told her the story of what had happened in Switzerland. She explained to Barbara that before going to Switzerland, she had acted like an orphan, not a child of God. She explained the amazing difference that comes into the life when a person sees God as a Father who loves unconditionally.

"Barbara was not hearing any of it," Rose Marie told me later. "She made no response but seemed reserved and cold to what I said."

Being with Barbara at that time was like sitting down to a meal with fish that has bones in it. You like the taste but are wary about what may happen with the next bite. Soon I found two big bones in my throat.

The first was our discovery later that summer that Barbara was slipping back to her old ways. We found a note on the dining room table that read,

Dear Mom and Dad,

I have gone to spend a couple of days with a friend. I don't feel well. Please pray for me. It is hard for me to ask this, but I have never felt so confused.

Love,
Barbara

For an hour or two Rose Marie and I were very upset. To us, "a friend" meant that she was sleeping with a man. But soon we cooled down. We sensed that we would have to take a stand against what Barbara was doing, but we knew it would be foolish to focus too much attention on it. Our first priority was to love her and leave the rest up to Christ. We were learning not to confuse our job with his. Since we could not change her, this was Christ's work alone.

When we questioned Barbara, she did not deny that she was falling back into her old ways. After some heated discussion with her, Rose Marie and I believed that we had to ask her to make a choice: submit to the standards of our home or leave. That was not easy, and we hated to do it. We were not demanding perfection and we could understand that she would naturally be tempted to slip back to her old ways, but she seemed to be saying more than that. She seemed to insist upon her right to her old lifestyle, which was something we could not live with. It was contrary to our Christian standards and something we would not permit anyone else staying with us to do if we knew about it.

So Barbara made her choice. She got an apartment about two miles away. This time, however, our friendship continued without a major breach. Once more the family pitched in and fixed up her apartment, cleaning, scrubbing, painting, and providing furniture. We have great children, and they have faithfully shown unconditional love to each other. More importantly, Christ was continuing to love Barbara aggressively.

101

But the second bone in my throat came soon afterward. I was standing outside our house one day when Barbara drove up. She was accompanied by a new young man. "Dad," she said, "I want you to meet a friend of mine, Angelo Juliani."

I must have poorly concealed my dismay. Angelo later told me, "Your face really fell when you met me. We could see concern written all over you."

Jill, Barbara's sister-in-law, was equally concerned. She told Barb, "If I were to rate Angelo among the men in your life on a scale of one to ten, he's definitely a three." Jill is a shrewd judge of people, and if Angelo could only make it up to three on a scale that included people like John, this did not bode well for Barbara's future.

What we began to fear soon happened. In early November Rose Marie reported to me, "Jack, brace yourself. There is a man's clothing hanging in Barb's apartment."

Happily I was braced—braced by grace. Again I had surrendered Barbara to Christ and, though concerned, was not worried. We had done all we could, and now it was up to Christ to guide Barbara to himself. I did not expect Barbara to end up in the abyss again, but if she did, Christ was the only one who could rescue her. And I was convinced he would.

Barbara's Response

I'm leaving you, John," I said as I threw my clothes and possessions into two big suitcases. At first he didn't believe me, but when I picked up the phone and asked my parents to come get me, he realized that I was, for once, serious.

"We can work things out," he argued. But I continued to pack without even bothering to reply. The surroundings were still beautiful. Spring had just arrived and everything was new and green. Outside stood our cars and big hunting dogs; inside I had plants, attractive furniture, and a beautiful wardrobe that took up a whole room. Still, I was leaving. John wondered why and so did I. Where did I suddenly get the strength to walk out on all of this? I didn't know, but I was happy that I had finally mustered the courage to get out of my mountain home and back into life.

My parents arrived and I left with them, sad and scared, but also relieved. I asked them if I could have my old room back. They agreed and I moved back into the corner room on the third floor. The only difference was that someone had hung a banner on the door that said, "How long, O Lord?" I ignored it and unpacked my things.

Immediately I began to reorganize my life. I went back to college to study political science and prepare for law school. To support myself I worked as a waitress in the evenings and on the weekends. My parents were convinced by all this activity that I had changed and would soon become a Christian. Actually, I had only exchanged my belief in happiness through self-indulgence for a new theory. Since hedonism hadn't worked, I reasoned that service to others must be the way to fulfillment in life. I knew my parents were happy and I believed that the reason was that they did things for others. Even though I didn't want to accept their religion, I intended to accept our family's strong tradition of service to others and success through hard work.

If my parents had known my thinking, they wouldn't have been so shocked when I started staying out all night with a new succession of boyfriends. At first I only did this when they were away, but since they found out about it anyway, I began to do so even when they were at home. My father and I had an unpleasant confrontation over the matter. He told me that he thought that I was wrong, (which was no shock) but he said two other things that made me very angry. First, he said that he thought that if I continued with this lifestyle that I would end up crazy, like a relative of ours who is a diagnosed paranoid schizophrenic. Second, he said that he was considering leaving the pastorate because of my behavior.

I thought these comments were intended to manipulate me into living the life that he wanted for me. I was hurt that my own father could suggest that I might lose my mind. *Even if it's true,* I thought, *wasn't the suggestion bound to have some power of its own?* For days afterward I struggled with fears that I was going crazy and I had nightmares that terrified me.

I also felt that to tell me that he might leave the ministry because of me was another kind of blackmail. *Why now, I* wondered, *instead of when I was living with Tom or John?* I told my dad I would be happy to move out because of our differences, but I would not change my behavior simply because he believed that it was wrong. I also told him that I didn't feel that it was his place to give me unasked-for advice about my personal life. "I have to learn by making my own mistakes," I argued. Once again I was making it very clear to my parents that their opinions were not something I wanted to hear.

I moved out, pretending to myself and to them that I wanted nothing to do with their old-fashioned morality. But at the same time, going from man to man was beginning to disturb me. I saw how little caring there was between any of us, and I began to distance myself from them all. Then I met a man that I really liked—Angelo Juliani. Outwardly Angelo seemed no better than any other man I had dated. He was a bartender at the restaurant where I worked and was not above stealing from the register or dealing a few drugs to make some extra money. He dressed in flashy clothes and platform shoes, and he wore his curly black hair in an afro.

I will never forget my father's face when he first met Angelo. Dad registered surprise and dismay as he did a movie-perfect double take. He said nothing, but his face was worth a thousand words. My friends were not as silent as my father, and they all told me that they thought I was making a big mistake. But Angelo and I were having a great time. His world was as foreign to me as mine was to him, but he was the first man I had ever met that wasn't intimidated by new experiences. Angelo was supremely self-confident. He wasn't even afraid or uncomfortable around my father! He laughed and joked with him just the way he did with his customers behind the bar.

We did everything together and had such a good time that it seemed natural for him to move in with me. It seemed that I had finally found the right path to happiness. I was working full time, getting "A's" in school, and living with a man that I loved. My parents and their whole way of life seemed very far away. I discovered that there were lots of people who worked hard and seemed happy and successful but weren't Christians. I respected my parents, thought they were good people, and enjoyed being around them. But I had no desire to live as they did.

When my mom told me about her experience in Switzerland, I was uncomfortable and bored. Angelo and I went to church once and neither of us listened to the sermon—we just left as quickly as possible. I was on a new path, and I had no intentions of it leading me to Jesus.

Chapter Nine

West Running Brook

*I*n his poem "West Running Brook," Robert Frost tells about a New England brook that runs west, unlike the other streams that feed into the Atlantic Ocean that run east. Despite heading in the wrong direction, though, this stream somehow winds and unexpectedly manages to flow into the sea.

God often works that way with us. He lets us head in our own directions, but when we get to the end of our meanderings, we are precisely where he wants us to be.

"Dad," said our meandering Barbara one day, "it feels right for me to be a waitress. I like it at the Block and Candle. I'm serving people, and I enjoy it."

Sitting to my right at the round oak table that dominates our dining room, she did sound satisfied. The meal was almost over. Across from me, Rose Marie was chatting with Keren, a sixteen-year-old, blond copy of her Nordic mother. In the background silver and dishes rattled in the kitchen as Aunt Barbara, Rose Marie's sister, put them in the dishwasher.

Barbara did not sound like the indolent princess of a few months back. Even from early youth Barbara had defined herself as having few ambitions and certainly no desire to serve others! So we were all ears.

"Tell us about it," I said. "I never thought waitressing would appeal to you."

"I'm learning," Barbara summed up, "that serving others has meaning for me. A waitress doesn't have time to think about her own feelings. You're forced to serve the customers the best way you can—the good and the bad—and do your best to smile when they complain or spill their food. It's something new and freeing. It's even helping me focus on my school work."

If the rest of us had heard this little speech from Ruth or Paul we would have nodded and said to ourselves, "Yes, that's the way they are," but from Barbara—well, it was mind-boggling!

That was the spring of 1978, about two years after Rose Marie's meeting with God in Switzerland. The change was remarkable. Two years before, in March of 1976, Barbara had caught mononucleosis and during the rest of that year had been so sick that she had come to us more than once to ask for prayer for healing. Now she was healthy. Her face was all smiles. Her sense of humor was back. She was tastefully dressed but without wearing anything that looked like it cost a month of my salary. She had left John, had her own apartment, supported herself by working in the Block and Candle, and majored in political science at Temple University.

Despite our hesitations about Angelo, we were delighted. Within two years, Barbara had overcome her self-centered lifestyle and was now relearning some of the habits of normal living. Of course, she was not yet a Christian, but she had broken with John, partly because of his intense jealousy, but also because she had begun to see that his way of life was simply wrong. More importantly, we had built a new friendship with her. Never again did Barbara view us as her enemies, which, I believe, was a major step toward her becoming a Christian. Without regaining her love for her family and her bonds with them, it would have been almost impossible for her to receive the message of Christ.

Her increased moral sensitivity prepared her in an important way to know God, for how can you ever see your need of Christ if you don't see anything wrong in yourself? Barbara had been deceived about herself to the point that she blamed others for her problems. Until early 1977, her conscience was so darkened that she could lie with a straight face and hardly know she had done it. If caught, she would self-righteously defend herself or tell another lie to cover up the first.

How, then, did God bring about these crucial changes?

One unusual tool our Father used was a local self-improvement seminar. At that time, that particular program was popular among Barbara's friends, so she and Angelo decided to attend some weekend seminars.

Barbara's biggest problem was game playing. Through our prayers she had had some awakening of conscience about it, but she still was a great blame-shifter. Yet in answer to our prayers, Christ used these otherwise secular self-improvement techniques to confront her—head on.

I would never have dared to do what the seminar leaders did, that is, to suggest to Barbara that each person is responsible for his or her own problems and has no right to blame anyone else.

On one of the weekends Barbara was in front of the audience doing a relaxation exercise that was supposed to get rid of headaches. Hers did not go away; the technique did not help her. But she knew what was expected of her, so she lied. Later in the day, she realized that one of her greatest problems was lying. The next day she went back to the meeting and confessed to the group that she had lied. The leader only nodded, but she felt a weight roll off her back. Our prayers for her deliverance from deception were being answered.

I could see changes in Angelo's life too, although I did not know all that was going on behind the scenes. Actually, I had decided it was better not to know. Suddenly, Angelo was showing the first signs of a conscience and began to talk about personal responsibility. He followed through by attending classes at Temple University with a view to becoming a public-school teacher.

By early 1978 Barbara and Angelo were strongly committed to one another and began to talk about marriage. I wondered what this would mean for me. Would they ask me to marry them—and what should I say? But for the time being they put off this decision.

The year that followed was a period of benign neglect on our part as parents. Barb's and Angelo's lives seemed to stabilize; both were getting outstanding grades at Temple, and a friendship began to form between Angelo and us. They came to all our family gatherings and seemed to enjoy themselves. In fact, Angelo was often the life of the party.

Let me explain that. The Miller children love to tell stories and anecdotes, so a family gathering often had a certain amount of competition to see who could tell the most fascinating or humorous story. When they were younger and more full of vim, a quiet person could hardly get the floor to talk. But Angelo had no trouble at all. He had a good sense of humor and his own line of anecdotes. He seemed increasingly at home with us in a way that Tom and John never had.

It was clear that the prayers we had first offered in Texas were continuing to have a powerful effect on Barbara. Around this time, when I came down with the flu, Barbara came into my room and sat down at the foot of the bed.

"My therapist suggested that you might like to hear some good news," she said.

"Please," I said, "I can always bear up under the weight of good news!"

"You know what a liar I am and how I deceive?" she said. "It goes back a long way."

I nodded, as I recalled the toothbrush incident.

"I'm with you," I said.

"Something is happening to me," she said. "I'm finding I can't lie any more. I hate to deceive people. And I'm beginning to see that that's part of the reason my relationships with men have been so bad. Recently I went down to the IRS and came clean about my income last year. It felt good. Somehow, I've got to take responsibility for what I do."

After telling her how wonderful I thought this development was, I asked her gently, "Well, now. How do you explain these mysterious changes?"

With a shy half-smile she said, "I think someone must be praying for me."

"Probably," I said.

This kind of bonding of lives through prayer made me feel secure in asking Barbara and Angelo to give me a hand on a project. In 1973 I had written (with a good deal of help from other Christians) a booklet called "A New Life." Now, five years later, I felt this evangelistic presentation of the gospel needed some revision. It seemed sensible to ask a number of non-Christians to help me make it more relevant in its language and applications to life today.

So I asked Barbara and Angelo if they would be willing to help me. I invited them to lunch and showed them copies of the booklet, pointing out areas where I needed advice on what people were thinking.

"What really troubles people today?" I asked them. "Here's what the booklet says; what do you think?"

After a few minutes, they came up with the same answer, really quite to my surprise. It was basically this: "Most people today don't feel guilty over the kinds of things that bothered your generation, but one thing gets us. We don't like being selfish and self-centered. That really bothers us."

The response was helpful. They even agreed to study the booklet further and to give me more ideas on how to make it relevant. Angelo, in particular, took an interest in this project, although I did not expect him to look closely at the biblical content. As it turns out, he did, and for the first time he began to understand something about the gospel and the biblical teachings of sin and grace.

As I watched their enthusiasm for this project grow, it occurred to me that perhaps these brooks would eventually find their way to the sea.

Barbara's Response

*L*iving with Angelo was an education—for both of us. With my new-found morality, I forbade his drug dealing and stealing. I had lived in fear of the law long enough. Angelo, for his part, refused to be taken in by the games I played in relationships ("take care of poor me"), and he encouraged me to stand on my own feet. During this period we started psychotherapy together. Since we wanted our relationship to last, we worked hard with our therapist to learn how to really care for one another. She suggested that at the end of our therapy we attend a local self-improvement seminar. She believed it was just what we needed to complete our understanding of human relationships and ourselves.

All my life (as my sisters and brother were happy to inform me) I had been a liar and a blame-shifter. In the seminar I came face to face with these traits for the first time. The first thing that happened was that I stood up in front of three hundred people and lied about having a headache disappear. I had volunteered to be part of an exercise that would show how will power can control physical feelings. With the technique, I was supposed to be able to banish my own headache. As I sat in front of this roomful of tired people (we had been in the same room all day and it was now 11:00 P.M.), I stared at the red carpet and tried to picture my headache leaving. The harder I tried, the more my head hurt.

113

Finally, in desperation, I said, "My headache disappeared." Everyone clapped in relief, and the seminar leader said, "You can see her whole face looks different."

I sat down amidst general approval, but I still had my headache. I tried to forget the incident, but my headache kept getting worse. By morning I felt like the top of my head was coming off. With the clarity that often results from pain, I saw that throughout my life lying had been my response to stress. I knew I had to admit to the people in the seminar that I had lied, even though confessing my lies had always been impossible for me. I went back to the seminar without knowing what to do.

In the bathroom before the meeting started, a woman came up to me and said, "Did your headache really disappear last night?"

I looked up and said, "No, it didn't!"

I ran from her shocked face into the meeting room and at the first opportunity, I got up and told everyone that I had lied. It was the first time in my life that I had admitted to a lie without being forced to do so.

My headache disappeared shortly afterward.

Confronting my habit of blame shifting came about in a less dramatic fashion. I had a long list of people in my life whom I could blame for every problem that I had ever had. During the seminar, the leaders argued that whatever you get in life, you've gotten because you really wanted it that way. As I listened to person after person arguing with the trainer, explaining how other people were truly responsible for the bad things in their lives, a light went on in my mind. For the first time I thought about what fun it had been to be the black sheep of my family. I was my parents' fourth child in four years, but with great adroitness I had managed to focus the whole family on me. With a sense of shock I realized that it was not my parents and their strait-laced ideas that were to blame for my unhappy life. It was me.

114

Through the seminars, I began to take responsibility for my life and work on personal integrity. Yet I was still ignoring God. I decided to donate some of my time to work in the seminar office. When I saw all the people that I had admired from afar relating to each other in this little office, I was shocked. When things didn't go well (which was almost daily) they cursed each other and told each other off. I quickly decided that this was not for me. I had seen my parents deal with people that upset them, and they worked hard at forgiving them and praying for them. No religion at all seemed better than this organization. I stopped volunteering and avoided any more contact with the people from the seminar group.

I shared these experiences with my parents. They were delighted that I was no longer casting them in the role of villains, and my whole family enjoyed the story about my lying. After all, they had known as far back as the toothbrush incident what I was like, and they were happy I had figured it out at last.

I was, for my part, happier now that I was lying less and blaming others less. I added all of this into my equation for what makes a life happy. Apparently, not only did you need to serve others and work hard, but you also had to act with integrity in personal relationships. At last I felt that I was beginning to find the path to lasting happiness and peace.

Chapter Ten

Deepening the Bonds of Friendship

*B*y the autumn of 1978, Barbara and Angelo were our good friends. Barbara had turned into a first-class waitress in a first-class restaurant, and her professors at Temple were impressed by her work in political science. They were already talking about graduate school. During this time, we had come to have great respect for Barbara, and we told her so.

Angelo too was doing well at Temple. We noticed his maturity, and we were especially impressed by his relationship with his father and mother, whom he honored by always speaking well of them. Barbara loved and respected them as well. Barbara and Angelo would spend Sunday afternoons with his parents, and Angelo and his dad golfed once a week. Obviously, Angelo was close to his father, a quality we admired, and we told him so.

At this point, some Christian parents might say, "But here you have a young woman, brought up in a Christian home, living with a man to whom she is not married. Won't they misunderstand your affirmations? Won't they think you approve of their lifestyle?"

The assumption is that non-Christians are not very bright—that they cannot distinguish between specific appreciation and general approval of what they do. I think that when Jesus ate with tax collectors and sinners he expressed by this act a qualified acceptance of them as people, but he was not endorsing their sinful patterns of living—nor is there any indication that the tax collectors and sinners interpreted his actions as approval.

It was the same with Barbara and Angelo. They were not stupid. They knew we disapproved of many of the things they did. It would have been foolish interventionism for us to tell them what we thought about their living together. They already knew.

Instead, we waited. Our patience was rewarded when they actually came to us to discuss their wedding plans. We listened sympathetically and prayed for them in private.

The changes in their lives were fascinating. Both of them were becoming honest in their relationships and trustworthy in their handling of money. They were developing more sensitive consciences, and the intriguing part was the way they helped each other to mature. Barbara, for instance, had challenged Angelo's drug dealing so strongly that he reviewed the whole ugly business and gave it up. Angelo, for his part, did Barbara the favor of refusing to accept her game playing. Before they attended the self-improvement seminars, he had already helped her see how she often blamed others for her problems. He saw that she liked to excuse herself by shifting responsibility to her parents or to the man she was living with.

When Barbara later described Angelo's method of handling her blame shifting, she had to laugh. "Dad, I love Angelo. He won't accept my game playing. When I try to blame him for my problems he just laughs. But he never rejects me."

"Barb," I said, "he sounds like a mature person to be able to do that."

Angelo was maturing in other ways as well. One time

Barbara asked me, "What do you think Angelo should do after Temple?"

As Barbara described his gifts and aptitudes, an interesting picture began to emerge. He was a good counselor, a good teacher, an able public speaker, and a genuine people person.

"Sounds like he'd make a good pastor," I said. We both burst out laughing. Knowing Angelo, it sounded incongruous, but . . .

At this point allow me to underscore certain aspects of our approach to Barbara. The key to winning a lost child, or any lost person for that matter, is to reach the conscience. The primary way to do that is by building a friendship based upon truth and love.

But to do this God's way, Christian parents must constantly work to rid themselves of negative feelings and attitudes toward the erring child. You cannot deny the past, of course, for you have been hurt—and hurt many times. You must learn to accept the past and not cram all these negative thoughts into the basement of your life, close the door, and deny them.

Crippled parents—those who have never had the basements of their lives thoroughly cleaned—will inevitably interfere with Christ's work in the child's life. Christ wants to reach the young person, to find that lost child, for he loves that wandering spirit. But the Spirit's convicting work will be severely hindered by a parent's unconscious rejection. The parent can have all sorts of bad memories festering in the mind and, as a result, close the eyes to the rebel's need for love no matter what he or she is doing. Parents, therefore, must cultivate their relationships with their own heavenly Father, because only from him can parents learn to forgive, bless, and love. So get in touch with our holy Father, keep in touch with him, and then you are most likely to learn how to get in touch with the wayward child and to keep in touch in a way that will reach the heart.

Ultimately, allowing God to love you is the only way you will succeed in showing love—tender love, tough love, patient love, seeking love, forgiving love, and "doing" love. Such love eventually triumphs. Sure, someone may say, "We tried all that but it didn't work, so we gave it up as useless." But there is another kind of love that I have already mentioned. It is *enduring love*. When your love is ignored or rejected, you keep right on showing love. Certainly you can't constantly chase the child around all the dark streets of life, but you can wait for openings; and when you see one, you throw the punches of love. Believe me, eventually some of them will land in the heart.

Why? Because enduring love is God's weapon for defeating sin. Enduring love is the same kind of love that God has for us in Christ. When he sent his Son to die for us, our sin could not be defeated by a stiff dose of law—only by an enduring love that paid the penalty of the broken law by a sacrifice on a cross. A key word in the New Testament to describe Christ's substitutionary work is "endurance" (Hebrews 12:2–3; 2 Thessalonians 3:5). He persevered to the very end in securing our salvation from sin, Satan, and death. He is the one who "endured the cross" for our sakes, while we ourselves were yet rebels against the Most High (Hebrews 12:2). At the cross he defeated my rebellion, and with this gift of his enduring love working in my heart, I can love my own child and thereby contribute to God's defeating sin in her life.

So my conscience was pricked by the Father's forgiving love. He captured my heart because he loved me and sent his Son to die for me when I was still his enemy (Romans 5:6–10). Such love was the only power that could penetrate the inner hardness of my heart. In turn, the believing parent can prick the conscience of the "youthful enemy" by continuing to express Christ's persevering love for the young person, a love that cannot be defeated by rejection, contempt, or even hatred.

But how do you practice this love? When should that love be tender? When tough? And when just friendly—just being yourself in a warm, open way?

By now Rose Marie and I had sorted out a good deal of this. When Barbara had been sick a couple of years before, we were very tender. She came to the door one day reeling with weakness. Rose Marie gathered her in her arms and took her to the doctor, where he diagnosed her sickness as mononucleosis. We cared and prayed for her at her request.

But we noted a pattern. Barbara would come home when she was sick from sinning and ask us for prayer. This happened a number of times. Finally one day Barbara showed up at the front door looking ghastly. I felt real grief as I took her in my arms and steadied her. Again, she wanted prayer for healing.

After a moment of thought I said, "Barb, I'm glad to pray for your healing, but something's wrong here. We pray for healing and you get well. Then you go and do evil things and get sick all over again. It's not right. This time I want to pray for God not only to heal you but to make you holy—so you won't want to live in your sins. Do you agree to let me pray that God will make you clean and holy?"

She nodded. So I prayed that the Father in heaven would make her into a holy person as part of her total healing. It was a sobering experience for both of us, and it had an effect on her life. She got well, and some of her old sins began to fall away.

But let me stress that the chief way that we showed love to Barbara was to welcome her and her friends into our family. Through the years we kept right on welcoming her and any friends she chose to bring. We especially tried to make them feel at home with us on special occasions like Thanksgivings, Christmases, and family outings. To many of them from a secularized American culture, our family must have looked like an extraterrestrial colony, citizens of outer space. Well, many of her friends looked that way to us too.

But we told them we were glad to have them in our home. We fed them, laughed with them, and tried to let them know that God loved them. Since the Bible teaches us that every person was originally made in God's image, we focused on treating her and her friends with respect and honor. In particular, we listened to their ideas, asked them questions, heard their answers, and sometimes disagreed with them. We also explained the spiritual basis of our lives and told them how we had become Christians.

What were we learning? That love is a many-splendored thing, full of compassion and passion? Certainly! But love at its essence is simply showing respect to others, treating them with dignity, and doing it whether the person is worthy of it or not. That was the gift we tried to give all our children, and we found that now it opened up the lives of Barbara and Angelo to us.

Actually this had an amusing side to it. The Devil in his efforts to destroy Barbara was putting her in contact with all kinds of non-Christians. But more and more she brought them home to us! A whole mission field was actually coming to our door. Between her college friends, her "glitter" friends, and her boyfriends, we did a powerful business for the King. Through her wanderings, all kinds of people were hearing the gospel and being touched by the love of Christ.

It was also excellent training for me, making me a better pastor and preparing me for hard missionary service in Uganda during some challenging days yet to come.

To get an idea of what I am like, you need to visualize me not only as a pastor, but also someone who is like a college English teacher. I enjoy books, traditions, culture, philosophy—a person who likes to spend time in the summer in Spain or visiting art museums. Before being a pastor, I taught high-school English in California and had several semesters teaching part-time in a university, not to mention my lengthy teaching career at Westminister Theological Seminary. I am also a westerner with a fairly rugged background in the coastal mountains of Oregon. My family owned a small cattle ranch there and my father worked as the government predatory animal hunter and trapper.

People like me often have some pretty conservative instincts. But Barbara and her friends were always there to help me break out of my shell. It was, in a word, salutary. I had to learn to unbend and depend on the Holy Spirit to show me how to distinguish between my own social prejudices and the principles that really mattered. Through the years I noted that many things I once considered matters of biblical principle were simply cultural accretions, practices that I had uncritically accepted as the will of God when, in fact, they were human traditions.

For example, I saw that there was really only one thing Rose Marie and I should forbid. It was that our house was not to be used under any circumstances for doing things that were immoral or illegal. We made this point clear to Barbara, and once that was understood, the air was cleared and we had no great conflicts. But this also liberated us to enjoy Barbara and Angelo in other ways that were good fun, like skiing or having a joyful home-cooked dinner with them.

I have a practical concern here for the Christian parent. Too often, we allow ourselves to be set up by the Devil, who loves to pin a negative label on us. He is very determined that the young people of our time see the Christian mother as a dowdy female joylessly attending an endless round of boring church meetings, and the father as a harsh, authoritarian figure who majors in nay-saying.

Therefore, we do not want to come across to our young people as card-carrying Christians whose lives are defined by dos and don'ts. We thank God that at times we had the courage to say no when everyone else was saying yes, but our fundamental calling is not to no-saying. Love is more open than that. It is willing to go where the tax collectors and sinners live and to do it with joy. Our aim must be to exemplify a holy difference—not to compromise with sin. And our chief witness lies in our joy. After all, the worldly Barbara could only pretend to be happy, but Christians have a joy that goes beyond words. Why keep it to ourselves?

Not long afterward, I had an opportunity to share this joy with a close friend of Angelo's who was being held on drug charges in a nearby detention center. Angelo and Barbara asked me to visit him. I did.

The prisoner spent the first five minutes telling me how religious he was. Finally, I gently but firmly summed it up, "Wayne, I'm sorry. Please don't try to con me. Everybody has his little games. I'll not play any with you, but don't play games with me either. If you want to be serious, I can tell you how to have a whole new life, one that is based on truth and love. Would you like to hear about it?"

For a moment Wayne looked angry. I thought he was going to argue with me. But then he began to smile and said, "Okay."

So I said, "Look, Jesus doesn't play games. He lived a life of truth and love. Now here's what he did to help us . . ."

Barbara's Response

*I*n the spring of 1979 an amazing thing happened: I actually accepted some of my father's advice.

Angelo wanted to get married; I wasn't so sure. I remembered my previous marriage and shuddered. While I was still going back and forth on this issue, I visited my parents. As we sat together on our back porch, I began to tell them about my plans to seek a doctorate in political science. My father said, "Four years from now you'll be twenty-eight. When are you going to think about having a family?"

My jaw dropped. I said, "Don't you think I should get married first?" Dad agreed and then asked me what was holding up my marriage to Angelo. This was the first time in the two years that Angelo and I had been living together that Dad had said anything about our relationship. Once in two years didn't seem like badgering, so I decided to give him a straight answer. I told him about my fear of failing at two marriages: "Everyone is divorced once, but twice?" Another concern was that Angelo didn't have a career and didn't seem to want one. When my dad told me that he thought Angelo would make a good pastor, I just laughed. But when he said that he thought our relationship already resembled a marriage and that we should publicly commit ourselves, I listened. Here, for the first time, I heard a hopeful note in my father's voice as he discussed my relationship with Angelo. My father's obvious respect for Angelo surprised me and encouraged me to think more seriously about marriage. I decided that for once I would take Dad's advice. So Angelo and I made plans.

At the same time, I was accepted into the graduate programs at a number of universities. I chose Stanford University in Palo Alto, California, and Angelo and I began to make plans to move to California. We decided to postpone our marriage until after our move since we had so many other things to organize before we left. Angelo was excited by the move but I was scared. I was leaving behind everything that made me feel comfortable. Although I knew I couldn't stay an undergraduate in college forever, I was afraid that I would fail at Stanford. What if I flunked out? I tried not to think about it. I packed my bags and kept my fears to myself.

In contrast to my fears and uncertainties, I was beginning to notice some surprising changes in my mother. I had listened quietly to her story about her experience in Switzerland a while earlier, but I hadn't paid too much attention. What got my attention, however, was the disappearance of her longstanding and almost crippling allergies. For years she had sneezed and blown her nose when she was upset, stressed out, or tired. Now for the first time she was walking around without used Kleenexes in her pocket. She seemed happier and stronger. When I asked her what happened, she said that they had disappeared soon after she had repented in Switzerland. Although this didn't make much sense to me, it startled me.

My parents' ability to grow and change is what impressed me most, even more than their constant love and concern for me and my friends. I had lived among non-Christians for a long time, and my experience was that most people get more bitter and more set in their ways as they get older. The opposite happened to my parents.

While my first inkling of this willingness to change was

when my father asked me to forgive him, I was beginning to see other changes in his life as well. His tendency to be impatient and irritable with others was dropping away. Now my mom was getting up early in the morning to read her Bible—without the box of tissues at her side. I didn't know how to explain these changes, but they stuck in my mind.

I knew I could, by an act of will, make big changes in my own life. But I wondered if they would reach the core of my being so that even my whole countenance would look different. My mom and dad had changed in that way; I wondered if Angelo and I ever would. I still did not question the path I had chosen, and I felt certain that a good relationship and a satisfying and successful career were the ingredients of a happy life. My main concern as I packed my bags for California was that I would not make the grade in the doctoral program.

If only I could get my degree—then I would be content.

Chapter Eleven

The Last Battle

Angelo stood up, wiped his eyes, and looked as though he might be trying to say something. Instead, he walked out the front door and stood alone for a few minutes on the front porch, having momentarily left the going-away breakfast for Barbara and him. We were also honoring Barbara for having received a fellowship to work on her Ph.D. at Stanford. Our living room was crowded with friends, relatives, and leaders from New Life Church.

Why had Angelo left? It had to do with a gift they had just received.

A short time before this celebration, it came to light that Barb needed another $500 for the move across the country to Palo Alto, and she just didn't have it. Neither did Angelo. They were feeling the pinch. What would they do?

As a result, Pat House, one of our deacons, had stepped into the gap. "Why not take up a collection?" he had asked. To get the ball rolling, he made a contribution, as did several of the elders at the church, as well as Angelo and Mary Juliani, Angelo's parents. The gift went well beyond $500.

I had just handed the envelope with the money in it to Barbara. It took her a moment to get it open. She did not seem to have any idea what was coming. When she saw it, she hardly knew what to say. Angelo was so struck by the love motivating the gift he simply sat on our couch—stunned. He was so overcome that he had to leave the room to compose himself.

This was an especially happy moment for Barbara. Both the gathering and the gift were our way of honoring her for the hard work that had brought her to this point. Her accomplishment was impressive. In high school she had been gifted but always satisfied just to get by. At Dickinson College she had not been an outstanding student. But now she had come through with remarkable success; she had worked almost full time in a demanding job, while studying full time at Temple, and she had come out with high honors. Then she had been accepted into the graduate schools of several top universities in the country.

In response, Barbara simply said with pleasure, "I'm overwhelmed."

Later, Angelo told her, "I never heard of a church with that kind of love. I was overcome. That's why I just couldn't stay in the room."

That night I was filled with thankfulness to God. I knew that he had moved the Christians in our church to have this kind of interest in Barbara. I sensed that our "love offensive" was coming into its final phase because now it was not just love from us. Dick Kaufmann, then a leading elder at New Life Church and now a pastor in California, and his wife, Liz, had taken a special interest in Barbara. They had visited her, been introduced to Angelo, and sought to be a friend to her. Dick had taken the lead in organizing the gift of money. And each elder and his wife there that morning had shown a genuine interest in Barbara and Angelo. Such a spirit of kindness had deeply touched them. And I was touched too and knew that Barbara and Angelo had some feeling that the love of Christ was reaching out to them through us. Their barriers and prejudices against Christians and the church were coming down—with a crash!

At our meeting on the bridge in Melrose Park two years before, Barbara had said to me that she wanted me to love her unconditionally. She was experiencing that love now—from me and many others. Barbara and Angelo suspected that our care was not from our own power or goodness but from Jesus, the King, who had taught us how to love others through his having loved us unconditionally. This morning's love was but a visible sign of the Father's grace. It gave me a great peace to know that the Father was now pursuing Barbara and Angelo, the way he had once pursued me and many other Christians. He had always been on their trail, but now it was overwhelmingly evident that he was their Great Pursuer. To use the imagery of Francis Thompson's poem "The Hound of Heaven," you could now hear "the beat" of the pursuing feet as they drew even closer.

Still, I was restless. I was satisfied that we, as church leaders and family, had demonstrated our love for Barbara and Angelo. Yet something was missing. Why did I sense that the last battle had not been fought, that it still lay ahead? What was left to do?

After that breakfast celebration, I knew that there was something painful Christ wanted me to do. Since so many prayers had been offered for Barbara and for us, I had confidence that Christ would keep me from my natural inclination to act out of my own self-will. So when one particular thought welled up in my mind, I was sure the next step was being made known to me by him.

It was a frightening thought—the fact that Barbara was *still* lost. Three years before it had been clear to her and everyone else that she was lost; morally and spiritually, it was as though she were driving her green Jaguar at high speed, in the fast lane, without any brakes. But now she was the soul of moderation and discipline. Order was touching all parts of

131

her life. Why even she and Angelo were soon to be married! The prodigal, or so it seemed, had come home.

But is moral reform—and social responsibility—the same as returning to the Father's home? Obviously not. Barbara was still lost, and without Christ she was going to hell forever. This conviction came to me as an almost irresistible compulsion. I knew that as her father I might be able to help her see that moving from outcast to social insider still left her life in deadly peril. But how could I speak to her about my concern? How could I reach her?

This concern did not actually hit me out of the blue. It had deeper roots. For some time before the breakfast celebration I had been praying for a Christian friend of mine. His unconverted brother had slipped into a coma and, so far as could be known, had died without coming to know Christ. This Christian friend and I shared this sorrow together. What did it all mean? Was it possible to become a Christian in a coma? Or to quote my Christian friend, "Will I only take my brother with me to heaven as a beautiful memory?"

We were heartsick at the thought and expressed our hope that somehow Christ had reached his brother in a way no one knew about. But his words haunted me as I thought of my own situation. Was this, in spite of everything, to be Barbara's end as well? I trembled at the thought. What a tragedy that would be!

If my love was genuine, I should be willing to confront her with the issue of life or death. It would be painful, and she might become angry and upset. But I concluded that if Christ was working in her life, then her initial reaction would pass away. If he was not working in her life, then there was nothing I could do anyway. I was convinced, however, that he was pursuing her and that now the Hound of Heaven was going to bite both. My belief was that through the pain of such an encounter, Christ would reveal his love for her and break the pride that left her prey to her own deceptions.

So in late August of 1979, I girded myself for the last battle. I committed myself to talking to her and telling her simply and forthrightly how it made me feel that she would not be with me in heaven. I humbled my pride and asked her to meet with me in our living room.

She sat in the chair next to the fireplace. I sat across from her. As I began, my feelings were mixed. On one hand, I was leaning on God because of my fear that I might say something foolish. On the other hand, I was filled with the compulsion of God's love to reach Barbara's heart with the truth about life and reality.

"Barbara," I said, "you know your mother and I are really pleased with how well you've done with your work and education. It's a great time in our lives to see you go off to Stanford and lay plans for a good future with Angelo. But there's a burden on my heart I feel I must share with you. It's simply that when it's all said and done, this life is soon over. I have been thinking that of my own life. And I want you to know that it seems so sad to me that when I go to heaven, I will only take you along as a beautiful memory."

I had meant to say a bit more, but when those last words came out, Barbara became very angry. Rose Marie, who had just come into the room, quickly retreated in tears. She told me later, "When I heard just a little of this conversation, I knew I couldn't handle it. I started crying and headed for the kitchen."

In her fury Barbara denounced me vehemently. It went on for several minutes. The substance of it was that I was always fighting with her, laying a guilt trip on her, and making her feel bad.

While she was going on, I listened, said nothing, and prayed. I prayed in confidence for God to touch her conscience with his Spirit, to convict her of sin, and to give her an awareness that it is insane to organize your life as though this present world was eternal.

133

Eventually she stopped. Again, I gathered my courage. "Why should it seem wrong for me to tell you what I really feel? And I do feel that way. I do not want to go to heaven and only take you there as a beautiful memory."

I hardly had those last words out of my mouth when Barbara blew all the fuses once more, with equal intensity. Again I prayed and waited. When she stopped, I said, "You're not right. You and I haven't been fighting all our lives. That's just false. I can only remember two or three fights when you were growing up—and you won them all. Really, we should have had more conflicts and settled some things. It seems to me that there's nothing wrong in what I just said. What's wrong with my telling you that I want you to go to heaven with me?"

The atmosphere was aflame with tension. But suddenly it broke. The look on Barbara's face changed. She burst into tears and came across the room and fell at my feet. With tears streaming down her face, she looked up and said, "Dad, we are going to have to do this more often." She laughed. I did too.

I held her and said, "I know, Barb. We must do this more often."

For several minutes we just sat there. Finally I broke the silence. "Barb, I want to ask you to do only one thing. Will you ask Jesus to reveal himself to you? Just that. Will you ask him to show himself to you?"

"I will," she said. "I want to. I'll ask him to show himself to me."

"That's all I ask. That's enough. He'll hear your prayer, I know he will. I love you. God be with you."

For me, the last battle with Barbara was over. I had been moved by the Lord to this final stage in his love offensive. Barbara's conscience had now been confronted on a deep level. I had no doubt that this was his work and that soon he would complete it.

Barbara's Response

*B*efore we left for California Angelo and I asked my dad to cosign a credit card with me. Since we didn't have enough money to get to California and set up an apartment, we were counting on some extra credit to help us out. Dad agreed to cosign and then said that he would see what else he could do to help us. We didn't pay much attention to him and continued with our plans for survival.

My family invited us over about a week later to a small gathering of friends and relatives who wanted to say good-bye. Angelo and I were shocked to see a pile of cards on the mantle for us to open. As we sat down and went through them, we found that we had been given more than eight hundred dollars. We were moved by the love that was showered on us by people we had often ignored and despised. Angelo in particular was undone. He knew that we had gotten something for literally nothing. We hadn't even been nice to most of these people, but even though none of them was rich, they had each given us substantial gifts. We had no way of explaining it, but we were grateful.

I have already mentioned my father's penchant for good-news—bad-news packages, and soon I found out that he did indeed have some bad news to go along with the generous gift. Since this was our last confrontation, it is etched in my memory. He sat in an armchair across from me in the living room where I was visiting my sister, Keren, who was lying sick on the couch. She remained a captive audience through our whole argument. As our voices got louder (or as mine did—no one else in my family shouts) she just buried her head deeper. At one point she looked up briefly to say, "I can't believe you guys are having the same old argument." She was right.

Our conversation began along well-established lines, but when Dad told me that he wanted me to go to heaven with him, I erupted in anger at the implication that I was headed straight for hell. I yelled at him about how bad our relationship was and how it would never improve if he was going to continue threatening me with hell. After I finished, he did something that changed our whole conversation and relationship. He stopped talking and just quietly looked at me. To this day I am sure he has no idea what an impact this had on me. Never before had I seen my father at a loss for words. I didn't know how to handle it.

"Had I gone too far?" I wondered. Something big must have happened to silence my father in this way. Suddenly, when I looked at that small quiet man across the room, I realized I loved him. I didn't want to hurt him anymore.

Finally he said, "I know you can't make yourself into a Christian. You can't become what you're not. Why don't you just pray that God will reveal himself to you?"

With those words the fight and rebellion drained out of me. He understood. I wasn't a Christian and couldn't change how I felt or who I was. I told him I would ask God to reveal himself to me and I did. When Keren sat up and asked for Tylenol, I went to find some with a sense of relief. I put the whole matter into the hands of God. If he existed, he would have to change me. I couldn't do it, and my family—no matter how kind and loving—couldn't do it either.

The next week Angelo and I piled all of our worldly goods in our beat-up green Datsun and headed for California.

136

Chapter Twelve

Home at Last

The letter was dated September 10, 1979. It was from Russell, Kansas. It said, in part:

> As we drive across Kansas, it becomes clear to us why Dorothy felt the need to hallucinate Oz. The road goes straight through the state, dipping slightly to accommodate stray hills. Angelo drives and I read aloud. Yesterday I finished *A Wrinkle in Time,* and now I'm reading *A Wind in the Door.* Angelo has never been read aloud to before and he loves it. I also love it. I get a chance to observe again the beauty of Madeleine L'Engle's writing.

Barbara was in a good mood. After arriving in Palo Alto, she and Angelo found a place to live, Barbara registered for her courses, and Angelo took a job as a waiter. We did not know it, but they also joined the feminist socialist movement.

Rose Marie and I were seriously considering going to Uganda for several months, beginning in late November. We had been invited to help establish a Presbyterian congregation there like New Life Church. It was a very big decision. As recently as August a missionary team had found Kampala brimming with hostility and gunfire, and when the members of the team found it prudent to return to Nairobi, their apartment was hit by a spray of bullets.

Many questions stirred in our minds. Do we have the courage to go to Uganda? Is it wise? People were being killed in the capital every night. Were we ready to face our own deaths? And most importantly—was it God's will?

As far as New Life Church, there did not seem to be any reason why we could not go. Ron Lutz and John Julien, by now well-established fellow pastors, had excellent gifts for ministry and were proven, dependable leaders. The church programs were going well. Dick Kaufmann had recently helped us elders to strengthen our whole organizational structure. Bill Viss, lately returned from ministry to Ugandan refugees in Nairobi, Kenya, was beginning to lead our evangelism program. I personally felt it would be good for the church and its leadership to be less dependent on me. But most of all I wanted our church to have a role in taking the gospel to Uganda.

After talking with elders, family, and members of the church, we decided to go if the security situation improved. Through telephone calls to Dr. Kefa Sempangi, a Ugandan refugee pastor who had been an elder in our church for several years, we learned that the security situation in Kampala had improved and that the hostility against Americans generated by the propaganda of former dictator Idi Amin was rapidly diminishing.

So Rose Marie and I flew to Uganda in late November, followed by a team from our church made up of David Powlison, Bob Heppe, Phil Gross, and Walt Kendall. Rose Marie and I had a brief personal struggle before we left. For me especially it was a time of soul searching, followed by a new surrender to the will of God and a release from fear.

Satan did not want us to go because he knew something we did not: that our decision would influence others. Out in

California, Angelo was watching us. One day he told Barbara, "I think I'd like to go to Uganda with your dad and mom."

Barbara was astonished. She could not believe it. "Ang," she said, "you'd have to become a Christian!"

"I know," he said. "I've been doing some thinking . . ."

Later Angelo told us that our willingness to die for what we believed played an important role in convincing him that Christ is a living person—which is a big step for someone considering Christianity. Our trip was also later used by God to lead Angelo and Barbara to rethink their relationship to the feminist socialist movement.

Before leaving for Uganda, I had a further opportunity to challenge Barbara to rethink one of her last, private fables. Through the years I had learned to listen to her and knew that there were many personal Oz tales she had believed. Fable number one was her casting herself in the role of the abused victim, especially as a victim of her parents and anyone else close to her. Fable number two was the idea that you could find happiness in the city of man without reference to eternity. I knew these fables were lies. I also knew they needed to be exposed, which is what had happened in our encounter in our living room back in Jenkintown.

By now I wanted to concentrate on fable number three. This concerned the notion that education has some kind of renewing power in it, especially education in an elite school setting. I simply wished to be Barbara's friend who served her by asking searching questions.

She and I had some long telephone conversations during the days right before we left for Uganda. I mostly listened. Essentially, Barbara was groping for the light while still resisting it. In particular, her conscience had become remarkably sensitized to the issue of integrity in learning and in the whole of life. She told me she was sick of being a phony. Her old line—that she was happy being a non-Christian—had died a deserved death. And graduate education was her last hope.

"For several years I've tried to reform myself, to be more honest," she told me on the phone, "but as an undergraduate at Temple it was not all that hard to piece together other people's ideas and come up with something that sounded original. In reality I was a clever borrower. That's not integrity. I can't do that in graduate school. I don't want to fail, but I'd rather flunk out than put together a lot of secondhand ideas. My problem is that I'm empty and really don't have any original ideas or the capacity to organize them."

There was a long silence. Finally I said, "Barb, what does it all come down to? I honor you for your integrity, and I agree it's better to drop out than to be a phony. I can pray for you, but it seems you need to get your case into a higher court. Think about it: Is there anything in graduate school that can give you this kind of integrity? Who besides God can help you?"

There was another silence.

"Are you expecting education," I asked, "to do what only God can? Have you ever considered that he's the source of all knowledge and wisdom?"

In Uganda I grew in my confidence that God was the Master Controller of all of life and of our family in particular. I trusted that he was putting together a program that would bring glory to him and salvation to Barb and Angelo. For the first time, my expectation was growing that God had big things in mind that would also include Angelo's salvation.

I loved the people of Uganda and the ministry I found there. Pastors Peterson Sozi, Edward Kasaija, Joseph Musu-itwa, and Patrick Kamya led us to a spot in Kampala between Owino Market and Kisenyi slum. Here we preached our hearts out. It was one of the most dangerous places in a dangerous city, but God worked powerfully through the pastors and our team. Rose Marie went with us, worked with the women in the Africa Foundation Orphanage, and at night we witnessed to the Asians and government leaders confined with us in the big International Hotel.

Rose Marie showed remarkable courage in witnessing in the markets and great graciousness in serving Christ in the church. She was most effective in presenting the Christian message to Asians in the hotel. Still, she found life difficult in Kampala. She was especially stunned by the inhumanity that human beings showed to one another during that turbulent period. White people were relatively safe if they stayed off the streets at night, but the poor Ugandans were victims of a city where law and order simply disappeared at dusk. The demons of disorder and revenge rode the streets at night. In the morning city officials would often pick up between twenty and thirty bodies of those slain the night before. Old grudges, bitterness, tribal strife, and murderous greed were the terrible heritage of the Amin years.

In mid-February we were on our way home. We flew into Kennedy International Airport, glad to be home with our family and friends from New Life Church. It was a joyous reunion.

In our family, God was continuing to display his winning methods. Barbara and Angelo were now married, and Barbara was in the position of having lost most of her illusions. Dorothy needed somehow to get back to Kansas—back to the real world. She needed help if she was going to have a marriage that worked, and she was now ready to admit she needed to have her sins forgiven.

Rose Marie called Barbara to talk about her Ugandan experience. "It's hard to imagine the disorder of this small country. At night you hear shooting, and in the morning the authorities may pick up the bodies left on the streets. But human cruelty took many forms. There was so much

141

indifference to the poor and orphans. In our hotel an Asian who worked for one of the banks was ordered out of his room, family and all, while recovering from a serious heart attack. It was because his employer was late in paying his hotel bill.

"In the hotel there was no water in the rooms much of the time, and you had to go down the hallway to take the yellow water out of the firehose to flush the toilet. Then when the water did come on, many people had left the plugs in the bathrooms and sinks, and the water overflowed into the rooms and hallways, causing the ceilings to weaken and sometimes collapse. Actually, I handled most of this okay. What was hardest of all was to see people's inhumanity. So many people were brutalized by the Amin experience, they only knew how to be brutal.

"My time there did open up some old wounds. When I finally arrived in Geneva on the way back from Uganda, I knew I had crashed in Uganda. It was a cultural shock to me, and I didn't have the resources to handle it. I became angry and withdrew. In Switzerland the dam burst. I cried and then finally asked your father, 'Why couldn't I love people more? What's wrong with me?' He just answered, 'Sometimes you act like an orphan—as though there was no Holy Spirit to help you. Don't you know that you are in partnership with the Father and that he loves you and wants to help you?'"

There was a long silence on the line after Rose Marie finished. Then very quietly with a choking voice Barbara said, "Mother, that's the way I am too."

Her mother's confession of weakness won Barbara's heart.

Not long after this conversation, Angelo said to Barbara, "Socialist feminism just isn't going to work. Everybody in it is so self-centered. No one's ready to sacrifice for it. An organization like this can only work if you're willing to give your life for it, like your dad and mom were when they went to Uganda."

A few weeks later we received an excited telephone call from our daughter-in-law, Jill. "Mom! Dad! Barbara's become a Christian! She's been trying to call you, but she couldn't get through. Call her quick!"

But this was not all the good news. Two weeks later, a second phone call informed us that Angelo too had become a Christian.

We were filled with praise! What else could we do but honor the sovereign Lord who bought them with his blood and had acted with such wisdom in bringing them to himself?

Barbara's Response

*A*ngelo adjusted to life at Stanford much more easily than I did. Soon after we arrived he had already found tennis partners and the best places for pick-up basketball games. He thought life in California was great, while I wasn't so sure. I was intimidated. I thought everyone I met was smarter than me, and I knew for sure that they were better read. The first-year graduate students argued about structuralism while I wasn't even sure what it was. When I had to give a presentation in my political-theory class, I was so nervous that I froze up. I was literally at a loss for words. In another we had to write papers and then Xerox them for the rest of the class to discuss. When my time came, my paper was ripped to shreds. I was devastated and sure that I would flunk out.

In desperation I worked harder than ever before. I spent all day at the library and worked through the evenings. I tried to build good relationships with my fellow students and professors. Every Wednesday Angelo and I would have a potluck at our house for students and professors. We began to get involved politically and we joined the New American Movement (NAM), a socialist-feminist group. We got together once a week and discussed ways that we could change the world.

Even as I began to feel more comfortable at Stanford, I was still sure that I was dropout material. I talked to my parents about my fears and my desire to have integrity in my work. I realized that throwing together papers that were a patchwork of other's ideas was not going to work in graduate school. After all, my professors' ideas were the ones I would have to use—they wrote the books I was borrowing from! As the end of the semester loomed closer, I panicked. As a last resort, I prayed—for A's.

When I got my grades I was shocked—it had worked. I received all A's. I and one other student had done better than anyone else in our first-year class. I breathed a sigh of relief and tried to forget that God had answered my prayers.

I still did not want to become a Christian, however. There seemed to be so many reasons not to. First there was Angelo. We were not yet married and I couldn't imagine giving up our relationship. I also did not want to become a Christian and then be married to someone who stayed home to read the Sunday paper while I went to church. Secondly, what would my new friends at Stanford say? How could I possibly keep their respect if I espoused an outdated Christian ethic? So I resolved to ignore the issue of God in my life. I had always underestimated myself and my abilities, and I decided that getting good grades was not an answer to prayer but simply an indication of my intelligence and hard work.

I worked hard at ignoring God and getting ready for Christmas. The only problems I had were a tension headache and the tendency to cry every time I heard the name of Jesus mentioned. I would hear the *Messiah* in shopping malls and I would cry. I watched the opera *Amahl and the Night Visitors* on television and I cried. Angelo just looked at me and shook his head.

When school resumed, so did the pressure. If anything, my courses were harder. I listened to my mother tell me about how she felt like an orphan and I knew that I was just the same. I opened the Bible and began to read through the Gospels. As I read about Jesus, I was overcome by his love for

145

people. I would sit in my kitchen reading the Bible with tears streaming down my face. As I looked at myself through the eyes of Jesus I became less concerned with what I would have to give up to become a Christian and more concerned with whether God would ever accept me. I finally saw myself as a completely self-centered person. My every good action was, I realized, selfish. While everyone at Stanford was praising me for the weekly potlucks, I did them simply because I needed to make friends and fit in. I saw clearly the motives behind my actions, and they all aimed at my own advancement.

Still, I could not rid myself of God's presence. Everywhere I went I felt that he was around me. I walked through Stanford's country-club campus amazed that I had never before been aware of God. One day as I walked to class, I began to think about a person I had wronged. I started to review the whole situation with shame and embarrassment. Suddenly it occurred to me that it was for just this stuff that Jesus had died. I no longer had to feel guilty for the way I was. Instead I could tell God I was sorry and be forgiven because of what Christ had done when he died for my sins on the cross. For the first time, the burden of guilt lifted from my back. I realized that whether I wanted to or not, I did believe in Jesus and had to follow him. I knew he was the way, the truth, and the life and I could no longer pretend otherwise. Surprisingly, I did not even want to.

I went home and decided that the next step was to tell people that I was a Christian. First, I wrote a letter to Angelo (we had gotten married a couple of weeks before) and then I called my parents. When they didn't answer their phone, I called my sister-in-law, Jill, and she told them. My parents called and right away my father asked me to pray with him on the phone. I wondered if he was testing me (old patterns die hard!), but I was happy to pray with him. All of us were ecstatic. Angelo came home and read the letter. He was supportive, but he had two demands. "I will never," he said

146

"go to church and I will never pray out loud. They're ridiculous!" I said that was fine, but I asked him if he would read the Bible with me. Since Bible reading was not on his list of ridiculous activities, we started reading the Bible together every morning. Often I would start my school work and leave him still reading in the garden.

On Easter Sunday Angelo's brother Larry insisted that we all go to church together. Larry was visiting us at the time and was no more religious than Angelo, but his idea of Easter was to go to church with his family. So we all went to the Presbyterian church that I had been attending. While Larry counted the panes in the stained-glass windows, Angelo was convicted of God's love for him. After we left the service, Angelo told me that he believed in Jesus. Several weeks later, after an intense struggle with his pride, he prayed out loud and accepted Christ as his Savior.

Chapter Thirteen

A Web of Glory

*T*he Sunday-school class was hushed. The senior-high young people were waiting to hear what Barbara would say next. She spoke slowly and with real pain. "I love you very much, . . . and I want all of you in heaven with me." Barbara was broken with concern over the spiritual coldness of some of the young people at New Life Church.

"Let me tell you about Jesus and his wonderful love," she continued. "You can learn from him. . . ."

The scene that followed was very much like the one that took place when I shared the same burden with Barbara five years earlier. When Barb spoke those words, some of the more indifferent young people were touched and began a painful rerouting of their lives to Christ. During the week, the first one came to her and made a commitment to Christ. Soon others followed.

When I told Barb I did not want to go to heaven without her, it had awakened her conscience to the issues of eternal destiny. And this awakening is still reaping results today. As I write this, almost six years later, Angelo and Barb now direct the youth ministry at our church. Whereas Barb was once cold to the love of Jesus Christ, she now feels the power of that love, both for herself and for these young people. It has been a momentous change.

To have even a small measure of sincere love for another person is a miracle. To have a big love for others is a sign that God's kingdom has invaded our world. It means that the revolution of God has come and that Christ has mounted a bold counterattack against the self-centeredness that has raged through our century.

Jesus, the Son of God, was the only one who could have revolutionized Barbara's life. The glory is his. He put the love in her life and no one else! The most important part that Rose Marie and I had was to learn to stay out of the way and to put our lives at his disposal to be used in ways often contrary to our own instincts. Christ captured Barbara in a way that highlighted her unwillingness to submit to him and our helplessness in changing her. Indeed, more than once he let us see that we needed to be rescued as much as Barbara did— perhaps even more, since there is no more impenetrable barrier to God's love than the sense of being right. So often self-righteousness controls a parent's attitudes toward a rebellious offspring.

For all of us, the power to change came from Jesus' pursuing presence. He took our humanness, failings, mistakes, and sins, and out of that unpromising mix he spun a net of love, a mighty web of glory that is still growing and changing many lives.

Consider some of the threads in this web. After Angelo and Barbara became Christians in the spring of 1980, Barbara finished her master's degree at Stanford and left the Ph.D. program to return home. She took a job as a teacher in Spruce Hill Christian School, where our son, Paul, was principal. Angelo began to study at Reformed Episcopal Seminary. These developments contained a certain amount of irony, for Barbara says she had two commitments as a teenager—never to teach in a Christian school and never to marry a seminary student. Within six months of her conversion she had done both!

When Angelo and Barb returned home, they had their work cut out for them. The pursued were now the pursuers, and they were soon to learn, as Rose Marie and I had, that death must precede resurrection. The first resistance they met came from our daughter Keren, who is five years younger than Barbara. One day in late April of 1980, I stepped into the kitchen where Keren was cooking dinner. I asked her what she thought about Barbara and Angelo becoming Christians. She thought for a moment and shook her head. Then she said flatly with a flash of her blue eyes: "Barbara? Yes, I think I can believe that she has become a Christian. But Angelo? Dad, how well do you know him? I do *not* believe it!"

I smiled and said nothing. But I thought to myself, *The King is on the move and many people are going to be astonished at his accomplishments. What's more, dear Keren, he's after you too.*

In God's wisdom, Rose Marie and I were back in Uganda when Barbara and Angelo arrived at our home in June. The shaky government of Godfrey Binaisa had fallen to a military coup. In May, therefore, we returned to Kampala to help nurture the fledgling Presbyterian Church that had recently been established there. We were also concerned about the safety of Kefa Sempangi, a highly visible leader in the now defunct Binaisa government. So we were not at home to greet Barbara and Angelo, but Keren was. In fact, she could hardly escape from them, since they temporarily moved into our house.

Immediately they discovered that it is usually easier to spread an illusion than to communicate the truth. For years Barbara had projected the image: "I'm happy. But Christians aren't." Angelo also had impressed Keren as a person who was "really with it"—a superior athlete, an outstanding dancer, a good conversationalist, and a competent bartender and

151

waiter. From the two of them Keren had caught the message that the glitter of the world is mighty sweet and only needs to be tasted to be enjoyed. By contrast, Christian women seemed to wear ill-fitting clothing and no make up, to devote themselves to having babies and washing diapers, and to spend any extra energy attending covered dish suppers and selling handicrafts to benefit the poor.

Now Barbara and Angelo could, in a sense, see in Keren a younger version of themselves, and they began their quest to communicate God's love to her.

They knew they had to teach Keren one fact first: that without God life in the world is boring. Keren also knew little about the intense fears that grip the inner lives of many sensitive non-Christians. It was too much to expect her to know that many non-Christians pursue pleasure because it is their only release from the pain of failed marriages and failed lives. Pleasure is the only anodyne they have to deaden their feelings of self-contempt and loneliness.

But after some trying experiences of her own, Keren too began to respond to the love of Christ. As Barbara pursued her, Keren began to rethink her values, and to her dismay she learned that the love of many non-Christians was only superficial, while the love of Christians like Barbara was remarkably enduring. At the same time, Bob Heppe, who had worked with us in Uganda, got to know Keren better, and he played a major part in her conversion. Before the year was out, Keren had entrusted her life to Christ. Bob later completed his part in this good work by marrying Keren!

Not only had Barbara come back, but eventually she was joined by many others. A number of her junior-high students identified with her and became Christians through her testimony. A couple of years later, Sally Osler, a longtime friend of Barbara's from Dickinson, began to visit us and stay overnight at our house. Sally is a lovely young woman, as fair as Barbara is dark. She gradually plied Barbara, Angelo, and

152

me with more and more questions about spiritual matters. Finally, one Sunday at lunchtime, I commented to Sally, "You certainly have asked a lot of questions lately. Are you getting any answers?"

After learning that she understood the good news of the Christian message, I asked her gently, "Well, what's preventing you from becoming a Christian?"

That question was greeted by a burst of happy laughter from Barbara and Sally. I am sure my face wore a puzzled look. "We're laughing," said Sally, "because Barb just asked me that question this morning."

That week, Sally gave her life to Christ. The web continually pulls in more people. I could go on and tell of others who found the grace of God through Christ's love working through Barbara and Angelo, but you get the picture.

It is a remarkable picture. After Keren married Bob Heppe, they went to Uganda for a time. I am writing this book in Malaga, Spain, and in a few weeks Rose Marie and I will join Keren and Bob in Dublin where we will be church planting together. Sally is now married to John Songster, a former member of our Uganda team. Angelo has discipled leaders among the young people much the way I discipled him after his conversion. A number of these young people have led others to Christ.

There is also Angelo III, almost three years old. Like Angelo and Barbara, he already shows athletic ability and not surprisingly, he has a great deal of bounce! He is a great entertainer too, especially for his younger brother Gabriel, now almost a year old.

This week Angelo was elected full-time youth director at New Life Church. He and Barbara now live with us in our large old home in Jenkintown with Rose Marie's ninety-six year old mother and Aunt Barbara, Rose Marie's sister. Angelo and Barbara have taken over a good deal of the outreach that we once had. They are a rare combination: they understand the Bible and its message of grace, and they also understand people.

What they have, and what Rose Marie and I continually learn from them, is how to be an example of people who love. They love much. They pour out their lives for the young people who come and sit before our fireplace in winter or sit at our picnic table in summer. Of course, Barbara and Angelo have struggles too. I feel for them when they see young people run from God and ignore the voice of Christ. They despair and get upset with the stubbornness of those they pursue. It is familiar territory. Many times you see how shallow your own love is and wonder if you love anybody in the right way. What is worse, sometimes the memory of your forgiveness by God becomes dim, and you begin to feel distant and superior to those you are pursuing. You can become a cold, professional hunter rather than a loving shepherd in pursuit of wandering sheep.

But Christ is always faithfully spreading his web of glory. In spite of our weaknesses, Christ keeps right on working. He constantly brings us to our many small deaths so that we may experience many resurrections. That's why it is a joy to live and work with Angelo and Barbara. Together we have been lost—and found again. All of us have been dead to God and his love, but now we are alive. All of us have been forgiven much. Jesus once said, "He who has been forgiven little loves little" (Luke 7:47). The other side of the coin is that he who has been forgiven much loves much.

Barbara's Response

My father talks about a web of glory that God wove around Angelo and me, and eventually reached many people. But anybody who met me soon after I became a Christian would be surprised that I reached anybody with the gospel. It was difficult for me to tell my colleagues at Stanford I was a believer. Even before Angelo became a Christian, people would back away in discomfort when he mentioned that we were reading the Bible together. We once had dinner companions who practically ran from the table after their "what's new" query prompted Angelo to say, "The Bible is." Reading the Koran would have gone over much better.

I knew, though, that my concern about other people's opinions was one of my biggest problems, so I prayed every day that I would be able to tell people what was going on in my life. Eventually I was able to share my new faith with many. Often I wasn't very coherent, but I plugged on.

I also discovered a new way of living. I had a peace and joy in my life that I had never experienced before. Even my studies, while still traumatic, weren't the burden they once were. I could take time now to enjoy the world around me—the flowers, the steady blue California weather, and the stars at night. For the first time I felt that I belonged in the world. I had finally found out that God, not me, was the center of the world, a knowledge that gave me the freedom to enjoy life. In class, as we nitpicked over Marx and Hegel, I could smile at the contrast between the knowledge I was acquiring at Stanford and the wisdom that God offers ("pure, then peaceable, gentle, and easy to be entreated, full of mercy and good fruits" [James 3:17 KJV]). As I saw how much I had to learn about God's wisdom, I decided that graduate school was no longer the place for me. After I completed my master's degree, Angelo and I went home to Philadelphia.

The next year was hard. God used the junior-high students at Spruce Hill to expose many of my sins, so that I had to relearn continually the major lesson of California—that Jesus died for my sins and no longer counted them against me.

As Angelo and I shared our lives with the young people at school and church, we learned the pain of the kind of unconditional love that God had taught my parents during my rebellion. I have often thought God has a keen sense of humor. How ironic that Barbara Juliani, the girl who would not give Christians the time of day, was now pursuing teenagers who felt the same way about her. For someone who loves to be liked, that is no easy task.

Although our life has not been easy, it has never been dull. The rewards have been greater than anything that I had while I was fleeing God, and my biggest reward has been our two sons. I always believed I would never have children, for I was too confused to know how to bring them up and I simply rejected the idea. After becoming a Christian, I realized that I was now free to become a mother. Although I had always rejected the idea of myself as a housewife and mother, I am now content to stay home and nurture my family.

Another reward has been the opportunity to see my husband grow and change. When we first became Christians I was always filling him in on the law ("no, Angelo we can't cheat on our taxes"). He was always happy to learn from me, and as the years have gone by God has deepened his understanding so that now he teaches me. He was always a nice guy, but somehow I never pictured him as the spiritual leader he is today. And then there's the fact that I had always sworn that I would never marry a pastor. Just the other day Angelo came in with the new business cards that the church had printed up for him. He proudly pointed out his title: "Youth Pastor."

Knowing Jesus has also brought Angelo and me closer to our families. Living with my parents has been a great support to us and a big help in our ministry to teenagers. Mom and Dad and I have never gotten along better. We enjoy living together, working together, and praying together.

Angelo's parents are also a big part of our life. He comes from a close-knit Italian family, who, like my parents, have always reached out to us with love, even as we kept to our own self-centered path. But soon after Angelo became a Christian, he wrote and thanked his parents for everything they had done for him, especially for their love and the high moral standards they set in their home. This was the start of a new relationship with them. When I hear friends complain about their in-laws, I thank God for mine.

Finally, it has been my great joy to see the love of God touch the lives of those around us. In particular, I am amazed to see how God calls those whom I had never dreamed would become Christians. My friend Sally was one of those people. She is beautiful, rich, and intelligent, and I have always been slightly in awe of her. I was so nervous about telling her that I was a Christian that I waited until the dessert of a long lunch to break the news. She didn't say much, but she began to spend more and more time calling me long distance from Harrisburg. After a couple of years she finally broke down and went to church with me. I was still amazed when she told me on the phone that she felt that God was calling her. I was even more shocked when she prayed with me later that night. Even though God has changed many lives over the years, I am still startled every time. After living for so long in a world where I only saw people get more bitter, I am still astonished to see God change people so that they are full of love instead of hate.

Eight years ago, if someone had asked me to list all the things I didn't want to happen to me, almost every aspect of my life today would have been on the list. It is true that we love a God who can do more for us than we can ask or think. I never would have picked this life. But I have never been happier.

Chapter Fourteen

Parents! Turn Your Problems into Opportunities

*J*ack! Look at Barbara!" With that shout, Rose Marie plunged into the swiftly flowing Smith River.

What I saw chilled me to the bone. Out in the water, our three-year-old Barbara calmly dog paddled, her small head half-submerged in the water. The strong current was quickly sweeping her downstream into deeper water.

I too plunged into the river. Moments later Rose Marie and I had Barbara safely in our arms on a little sandy beach, and I tried to explain to our daughter that this northern California river was dangerous. It didn't register. In her mind the "swim" had been enjoyable—so why all the fuss?

This early rescue was an appealing parable of our mistakes in our later pursuit of Barbara. It dramatizes the way we wanted God to help us rescue her. We wanted to dash into the water, pull Barbara out, and hardly get wet in the process.

That, as you have seen, is not what happened. We could not be Barbara's lifeguards. Only our heavenly Father can do that, and he did it in a marvelous way. We played a role in her rescue, of course, but God never allowed us to get more than knee deep in the shallow water.

Furthermore, we came to understand that we too needed

rescuing. Barbara was not the only one who manipulated people. It is not hard for a parent to see through a rebellious adolescent's stratagems for getting and maintaining positions of power in the family, but it is another matter when you, the parent, have to confront your own manipulative techniques of consolidating power.

The primary game that parents play is so built into the parental mindset that only grace can release the practitioner from its bondage. That game is *control*. The controlling parent views the child as a possession, almost as an extension of the parent's own personality. Control is the effort of parents to exercise a godlike government over the child's life. Often unknowingly, they want the power to shape the child in their own image, without respect for the integrity of the child's own conscience. Parents often feel they must control the child to protect their own reputations. The child's failures, they believe, are the parents' failures.

Nevertheless, this assertion of the parental will is an act of rebellion against God who alone has ultimate ownership of and control over the child. Yet this rebellion is difficult for parents to detect. Many parental interventions are right and good in themselves. Without prompt action, for example, Barbara would have drowned in the waters of that northern California river. Any child who is not firmly disciplined and lovingly nurtured by his parents will likely turn into an adolescent monster. Effective parenting *does* require a certain amount of parental rule, especially in the early years.

But control is another matter entirely. It is dangerous because the parent who practices it omits something essential. Many fathers and mothers are simply more satisfied with a child's conformity and less concerned with the youngster's motivation and hidden desires, with what the Bible calls "the thoughts of the heart." Often unconsciously, the self-centered parent labors to form an orderly child who performs well in public and does not shame the family by disturbing the status quo. The problem, of course, is not with the orderliness of the child but with the shaping of a person with a desensitized conscience, a performer who has never learned to love God or people from the heart.

Open any of the gospels and you see the end product of this emphasis on conformity—in the behavior of the Pharisees. Jesus calls them hypocrites, which literally means "play-actors."

When control becomes successful in Christian families, a whole generation of hypocrites comes into being. These play-actors may seem to serve the church faithfully; they may even establish outwardly good families themselves. They can carry on the traditions of the faith. Unfortunately, they can gain the reputation for knowing God while their hearts are like that of the elder brother in the parable of the lost son. Although his body stayed home, his heart was far from the father and his joys. In some ways the elder brother was more lost than the younger, and what was worse, he was unaware of it.

More commonly, however, control stimulates rebellion. You may say to your child, "Come to Christ," while your actions and attitudes may say something quite different. You may actually be communicating this: "I want you to think and act like me, be orderly like me, be a carbon copy of me." In such circumstances an invitation to come to Christ will sound to the young person like a call to give up his or her identity, and it will be read as a call to be mastered by the parent rather than by Christ. For the child under a Christian parent's control, salvation means the loss of identity. Given such prospects, what young person would want to be saved?

According to the Bible, the human heart "is deceitful above all things" (Jeremiah 17:9). It even practices self-deception. I know that I have often unconsciously tried to control my children not for the glory of God or for their spiritual welfare but for the sake of my own peace of mind and reputation. When you as a parent persist in this mistake, you end up with

161

an overload of the wrong kind of conflicts as the child grows older. You will be caught up in an endless power struggle with the self-centered ambitions of the adolescent clashing with your own love of dominance. In despair you may take up the game of "innocent victim" as more suited to your experience. Since your control has been rejected by the child, you now see yourself as the holy martyr, suffering at the hands of your offspring because you have taken a stand against a rebellious child and a self-centered youth culture.

One fact should be clear by now: none of us is innocent. While the prodigal son's rebellion was evil, the elder brother's more subtle rejection of God was every bit as bad. As parents, we fail in many ways we never see. Even though each person is responsible for his or her own sins, a parent's sins can damage children. So in conflicts with your offspring, beware of being overly innocent. Don't live a lie or deceive yourself about your own failings. Children play their games; parents play theirs—the games of control and pretending to be the innocent victim. Not to admit our game playing, to insist at all times upon our own innocence, is to embrace what psychologists define as neurosis. Arthur Miller once wrote that the most innocent place in any country is the insane asylum; "There people drift through life totally innocent, unable to see themselves at all. The perfection of innocence, indeed, is madness."*

As Christians, we routinely acknowledge that we are all sinners. We may not all be *lawless rebels,* but it is nevertheless true: we are all tainted with sin. How? By our inward rejection of God's control over our lives. We continue to try to take over, to run our own race, to be our own boss. Sin is not just doing bad things like dishonoring parents, lying,

*Arthur Miller, "With Respect for Her Agony—but with Love," *Life* 55:66 (February 7, 1964).

cheating, stealing, or committing adultery. It is also saying to God, "No, you cannot rule over me. I will rule over myself and my family, and I will depend upon myself and not upon you to train my children. You can assist me from time to time when things are desperate, but I will not permit you to take full control."

But the discovery of our sins presents a great opportunity. Our instinctive reaction is to feel threatened and defend ourselves, but that is to miss the opportunity to know God by taking a radical step that will revolutionize both your own life and, in time, your family's.

Consider how unsatisfying much of your life is at present. You long to be a better person and a better parent, but you can never quite achieve that. You may even have to admit that as a parent you are often obsessed with your own anxieties, pains, and failings. Driven by frustration, you may go from book to book, from counselor to counselor, trying to find the how-tos that will turn you into a successful father or mother. But the difficulty does not lie with the counselors or the books on family life and child training; it rests with you.

What is the real problem? It may be that you simply do not know as much as you should about God's grace. Maybe you know nothing at all about it.

But that is also your great opportunity. Grace is available for those who have a knowledge, a faith-awareness, of their deepest need, a need that is the same for all human beings, but so long as we are successful in all aspects of our lives it remains a need that we are not conscious of. Rose Marie and I encountered this same opportunity in our long, slow, uphill struggle to reach Barbara as we discovered again and again that you cannot rely on anything in yourself in this undertaking. The knowledge of our own inability brought us closer to a true experience of grace.

Gradually we came to see that our need for grace has two sides:

1. a knowledge of God's unconditional love for me as a child of God, adopted into his family on the basis of personal trust in his death for my sins (Galatians 4:4–5);

2. the continual surrender of my life to the control of the Spirit of the Son of God, to move from thinking like an abandoned orphan to confident trust in the Father (Galatians 4:6).

Rose Marie had been led by God into such a commitment through her encounter with him as a forgiving Father in that Swiss communion service. She put her faith in Christ's sacrificial death for her on the cross, and God assured her that he had pardoned her sins and accepted her as one of his dear children now and forever. At the same time, he enabled her to begin to surrender her life to the control of the Holy Spirit.

Before this work of grace, Rose Marie had been more of an observer watching me pursue Barbara. She watched with love but, to quote her, "with the helplessness and sense of defeat that goes with the mind of an orphan." After the Father's extraordinary encounter with her, she reported that she had a fresh sense of forgiveness herself and was able to do the following:

1. To trust in God's control of Barbara and not attempt to control her by her own maternal self-effort and will power.

2. To reject the notion than she was a helpless victim, a wronged orphan forgotten and unloved by the Father.

3. To develop strong confidence that God has a perfect plan for our family and for Barbara.

4. To pray for Barbara with new authority and particularity, by claiming the promises of grace in the Spirit of sonship, and see Barbara begin to change as a result.

5. To endure the pain as a parent and keep on with a love offensive even when it seemed to produce few results.

6. To deepen and enrich her friendship with Barbara by a spirit of openness and unconditional love.

7. To grow in her ability to speak to the conscience of Barbara and others through learning to listen, ask questions, and apply the Scriptures concretely.

8. To support me in prayer when Barbara and I went through the climactic last battle that brought her over the final obstacle.

So our story comes to its climax with this perception: What seemed to be a tragic defeat for us as parents turned into an unprecedented opportunity to grow and mature as Christians and to learn extraordinary things about God and his ways.

If you struggle with a rebellious child, ask God to show you his view of power in human relationships. From him you will learn that the power of God does not consist in the capacity to control others or get your way by playing games. Instead, it begins with the release of love as you forgive your erring child. It expresses itself in the capacity to endure when your love is ignored or even rejected. It is the power to mount a love offensive by doing good right on the heels of your being wronged. It is also the power to confront sin with tears and great humility, and wait until one day when you see a familiar figure coming down the road toward home. Then it becomes the power to go forth and welcome home unconditionally the one who was lost, the power to celebrate with the angels the return of the lost son or daughter.

Obviously none of us has this power within ourselves. You cannot work up enduring faith and love from the human spirit. But Christ gives it to those who are willing to abandon their own innocence, their own control, their own precious self-pity. Humble yourself, submit to him, and ask him for grace in your deep need. Ask him to reveal himself to you. From him claim full assurance that the Son of God took away all your sins and changed you from an orphan to a son.

Then reread this book and see how you can learn from it to mount your own love offensive. I have no doubt that the Father will do for your prodigal what he did for us and our daughter Barbara, and the many people who have also come with her and Angelo into the Father's house.

Barbara's Response

*W*hen I first told my parents I wasn't a Christian, I think they expected God to deal me some grievous blow to make me see the light and come running home. I often felt, with irritation, that my parents and the Christian community were praying for catastrophes to bring me up short. Many painful things happened to me during this period, but the work of the Holy Spirit was to gently lead me from darkness to light.

Looking back, I picture my life as the big living room in our home. At night, when I first enter the room, I quickly turn on the light so I can see. But the room is so big that as I go forward I have to keep switching on lights. It is only when I reach the other side that the whole room is illuminated. In my life, God turned those lights on for me and then guided me to the next lamp. If he had turned them all on at once, I don't think I could have endured the brightness on the messy life that would have been revealed. Instead, God showed me the truth about myself bit by bit, in pieces that I could handle. In this last chapter, I want to talk about some of the lamps that God switched on that eventually led me to the Light of the World.

As a teenager, I experienced deep insecurities and anxiety. At first I attributed my depression to my parents' "shoving Christianity down my throat." I believed that what I was lacking was the fun, excitement, and material things the world had to offer. But after collecting and discarding a husband, a live-in lover, several houses, clothes, jewelry, a fleet of cars, and sixteen Rhodesian Ridgebacks, the first light went on in my mind. I realized that the way to happiness was not through hedonism. I had tasted what the world had to offer and I was no happier.

The next lamp that God turned on for me had to do with my own responsibility. Up until the time of the self-improvement training, I firmly believed that others were to blame for who I was and the bad things that had happened to me. (I never had trouble taking credit for the good things.) My whole life had a different focus when I realized that I, not my parents, friends, or lovers, was in charge of my own feelings and actions. I still had a lot of anxiety and depression in my life, but I no longer thought that others were to blame.

By the time I went to Stanford, I was thinking more clearly in many areas, but I still believed that if I could change my external circumstances, I would be a happy and peaceful person. I was no longer focused on adolescent fantasies of material wealth and happiness. Instead, I had an adult fantasy that included success and making an impact on the world. It was a great shock when the next light came on in my life and I realized that even fulfilling this new dream would not bring me happiness. I remember writing to my sister, Keren, saying that even as I pictured myself wearing a tweed suit, speaking insightfully to groups of wide-eyed students, and writing books of great worth, I could see that underneath I would still be the same old Barbara—fearful and anxious about everything. At last I saw that changing my outside would not change my inside.

The last lamp that illuminated the whole room of my life showed me what I was really like. Only then could I see that my fears were rooted in my self-centeredness and my broken relationship with God. Augustine talks about a void in man's heart that is shaped for God and nothing else. I saw that I had been trying to fill that void with things and activities, some good and some bad. I kept wondering why I wasn't filled up by all that I acquired or did. At last I realized that only God could meet my need for him. Even now, as I occasionally stray from my first love, God keeps reminding me that my deepest need is to have a right relationship with him.

There have been many benefits in writing these responses to my father's book. Certainly the most important has been the chance to review and remember all that Jesus has done for me and for my family. Not to be taken lightly, though, is the chance I now have to end this book and, in so doing, to have the last word. Here it is:

Thank you, Mom and Dad, and thank you, Jesus.